School's Out

JEAN BENDELL

School's Out

EDUCATING YOUR CHILD AT HOME

ASHGROVE PRESS, BATH

First published in Great Britain by
ASHGROVE PRESS LIMITED
19 Circus Place, Bath BA1 2PW

ISBN 0 906798 77 9 (paperback)

First published 1987

Photoset in 11/12½ Bembo by
Ann Buchan (Typesetters), Surrey
Printed in Great Britain

TO
VICTOR, HOSANNA, FIORIN AND TALIESIN

Acknowledgements and thanks

to our friends – Jean Dickens, Patricia and Mervyn Webb, Meg Roberton, Rebecca Wilcox, Judy Noke, Georgina West and Heather and Brian Hayward – for all those conversations about education, echoes of which they may see in the pages of this book

to Primmy Chorley, Betty Ball, Jude Ashley-Walker, Leslie Downie, Rena Laslett, Wendy Razzell and Nick Everdell – to whom I am particularly grateful for allowing me to include their accounts of home education

to Education Otherwise, to the General Secretary, Joan Hoare, for permission to quote from E.O's publications

to all the editors of the Education Otherwise newsletters and of *School Is Not Compulsory* – their work made my work so much easier

to the many people who have answered my letters and questions, and to all those from whose writings I have quoted: among others, Sylvia Jeffs, Lynette Cameron, Diane and Andy Anderson, Bruce Wallace, Antonia Young and Jill Gillings

and to Victor for all his help, support and involvement, not only with the writing and editing of this book but also with the idea and reality on which it is based, the education and upbringing of our children.

CONTENTS

		page
Introduction		9
CHAPTER ONE	Early Plans	11
CHAPTER TWO	The Five Hundred Days	19
CHAPTER THREE	We Contact the L.E.A.	30
CHAPTER FOUR	Our Reasons – Practical	40
CHAPTER FIVE	Our Reasons – Political	52
CHAPTER SIX	Our Reasons – Poetical	66
CHAPTER SEVEN	Obstacles and Objections	78
CHAPTER EIGHT	Home Education and the Law	100
CHAPTER NINE	Different Approaches	117
CHAPTER TEN	How Home Education has worked out for us	136
APPENDIX I	A History of Home Education	154
APPENDIX II	Education Otherwise	175
APPENDIX III	Resources	178
Bibliography		193
Addresses		196
Index		201

Introduction

Over the years, many people have expressed surprise and interest on hearing that my two daughters learn at home. Not everyone is aware that home education is a legal alternative to school. One of the commonest questions we are asked is, 'Are you allowed to do that?' Even when we assure them that the law allows parents to keep responsibility for the education of their children, some still assume that we must be battling with the Local Education Authority to exercise our rights. Yet we are just one of a growing number of families whose children are happily learning at home, without legal conflict.

Another question that we are sometimes asked concerns the practicability of learning outside a classroom. How, for example, do we manage to fit in all those long hours of daily teaching that many people assume will be necessary to parallel schooling? We have found that children can, and do, learn at home successfully within the normal family framework. This form of education does not cost a great amount and does not necessarily require the resources and specialized skills that many people might imagine. And it does work.

When I sat down to write this book my first thoughts were to ask myself what it was I had to offer other people who were contemplating education at home. I do not have any higher qualifications nor have I had a teacher's training. I hope that what I have written will offer encouragement to other parents who wonder whether they have the means to cope: you don't have to be highly qualified, well-to-do or living an alternative lifestyle. You do need to care – to care about the quality of your children's lives, their education and their future.

This book is about home education, not about the faults and failings of the school system or of teachers, individually or collectively. Inevitably, there is some criticism of schools and teaching methods. However, I did not set out to catalogue the iniquities of schools but rather to show the benefits and possibilities of learning in a family environment.

Being the mother of daughters, I have found it less complicated to use feminine pronouns throughout, except where I am specifically writing about a man or boy.

1

Early Plans

My two daughters, Hosanna and Fiorin, have been learning at home since they were born. Like a number of other children, past and present, neither of them has been to school.

The decision to educate our children at home – or let them learn at home, as I see it now – came about in two quite separate stages. First, there was an early, idealistic plan which gave me the basis, the underlying principle that there must be a better way to prepare young people for life than the process that I and my friends at school were being put through. Of course I had no experience of parenthood at that time, only an experience of the education system. The arrival of Hosanna eight years later put paid to much of my early theorizing. It took me a while to get used to the realities of life with a small child – not at all what I had expected – and, by the time I had, I found we were on a path that seemed to lead directly towards school.

The second stage came when Hosanna was three or four years old, when primary school was looming on the horizon. It was now that the decision about her education could properly be made – based on real life with a child rather than on an idea of how life with children should be.

But, first, those early plans: I was sixteen when a friend gave me a book which she urged me to read. The book was *Summerhill* by A.S. Neill. I remember expressing surprise – what would I want to read a book about children for? – but she assured me I would find it interesting.

I read it and had my view of child-rearing altered virtually overnight. I saw for the first time that bringing up children did not have to be the dreary business I, at sixteen, had assumed it to be. I saw something generations of people had seen before me – that there are dynamic possibilities in parenthood, other ways of bringing up children, other things to consider apart from the necessities of keeping them clean and clothed and fed. I made up my mind then that I should like to keep full responsibility for their upbringing and education.

My plan was that my future children would not need to go to school but would learn all the valuable things that school could teach them – and plenty that school would never teach them – through being with interested and interesting people. It seemed to me that many of the facilities generally provided for children – school being the most obvious example – limit their access to the wider world and effectively keep them locked in what seems to be a child culture but is largely an adult creation.

Although it was reading *Summerhill* that prompted this sudden awareness, the resulting plans bore little resemblence to A.S. Neill's splendid down-to-earth philosophy. Re-reading the book some years later I realized that *Summerhill* worked on me like some sort of catalyst. The ideas that crystallized in my mind were not a logical extension of his arguments. Summerhill was a boarding school after all, albeit a progressive one. I must have been reading into the book what I wanted to find. What I came up with was my personal view of parenthood.

There were certain aspects of Neill's ideas that I drew from. I found his arguments for self-regulation very persuasive. But I thought that the environment could be such that children did not only have the prevailing culture to choose from. It would always be there, of course, but if children were also shown other ways of looking at life it seemed to me they would have more choice. Neill advocated children choosing freely for themselves. He felt that they chose, and should choose, their own world. He pointed out that the children at his school enjoyed popular music and television. My feeling was that they only made their choices from the world as they experienced it. If the children at Summerhill were bombarded from the cradle on, as are most children today, with the all-pervasive television culture then, in choosing that, they had little more real freedom to choose than the next person.

Summerhill helped me to see that the way we bring up our children is an integral part of our life and beliefs. To me that meant it could be a poetic rather than a prosaic experience – an act of creation in a wider sense. Not long after this I had a dream. The dream was very simple – that I was going to have a daughter and that I should call her Hosanna. I had never heard of Hosanna as a name (though it was in use from the beginning of the thirteenth century) but that was that matter decided.

I envisaged a family of children brought up in what I felt had to be a rural setting, away from the many pressures to conform to other people's expectations. W.B. Yeats's 'acre of stony ground, Where the symbolic rose can break in flower' described my ideal. For myself I saw the role as Yeats describes:

> Having inherited a vigorous mind
> From my old fathers, I must nourish dreams
> And leave a woman and a man behind
> As vigorous of mind.

With all the arrogance of youth, I assumed that I had plenty to offer my children in terms of mental vigour, and that my main task was to 'nourish dreams'. This seemed much more important to me than their intellectual development.

Hosanna was born several years later when my husband, Victor, and I were living in a rented attic flat in a Georgian house in Bath, a far cry from my vision of a rural environment. She was born, not only on the very day she was due but also weighing exactly what I had predicted – 8 lb. Although labour had been long, the birth itself went rapidly and smoothly. Within minutes of being born, our new daughter lay looking first at her own fingers and then, it seemed, seriously taking note of all around her. She had a mass of dark hair and smooth skin – a great beauty to our eyes. I felt wonderfully blessed. I thought I was at last comfortably settling into my idyll.

The day after the birth the departure from the idyll began. This dream child of ours inexplicably started crying, more like screaming, for long periods of the day – every day. It was quite unlike anything we had expected. She seemed as if she must be in pain. Even the midwife said, in all her years as a nurse she had never come across such a 'bad-tempered' baby. The doctor murmured something about colic but also said experts thought the condition did not really exist. He suggested that I should start drinking stout as this could have a calming effect on breast-fed babies and even joked that I should put a teat on the beer bottle.

However much we tried to comfort her, however much we rocked her and cuddled her, whatever we did, she would not stop. She would sleep fitfully for only a few minutes at a time but would wake again very suddenly, screaming furiously as if in pain. I tried doing it the 'primitive' way, putting her in a baby carrier so that she could be soothed by my heartbeat and movements while I worked . . . it made no difference. I remember washing the dishes and cutting up vegetables with this poor, screaming infant attached. I tried switching her from my front to my back. It was then that it struck me there was something almost ludicrous about this, a woman working with a screaming appendage – did this ever happen to the Yequana Indians? At night, when she was a few weeks old, the screaming went through from seven in the evening until seven the next morning with one or two short breaks of a few minutes. She became really quite hoarse but still did her best to keep going.

We were dazed by it all – how could it be? This was nothing like the dream of motherhood that I had imagined. I have looked at books on babycare that suggest that newborns sleep for twenty hours out of the twenty-four, that demand-fed babies who are carried about by mother never have any cause to cry or – conversely – that it is possible to 'leave baby to cry herself out'. What we were going through was not even acknowledged as a possibility. I found myself secretly looking up autism and brain damage in medical books.

Then suddenly it did end. We were never more amazed than to find ourselves, about a month later, with a visibly cheerful baby, still very wakeful but no longer in whatever pain had caused all those weeks of screaming. She still slept for shorter periods than I would have liked but at least at night she slept for hours at a stretch rather than minutes.

That early difficult period affected my expectations of motherhood. It showed me that there were times when theories simply could not be applied. I had believed that it was perfectly possible to paint, write or pursue whatever adult interests you wished while being responsible for the care of young children. I had not realized the degree of determination this would call for when the children were very young. It can be done, I am told, given support from other adults (or babies who sleep!)

Not everybody has the same experience. I have often been amazed when passers-by have looked into the pram and said something like, 'Enjoy it while you can. They get worse as they get older.' I often wonder what sort of babies they could have had themselves – certainly nothing like either of mine – or why they experience their children as being so terrible. I find life with children gets easier as they grow older (though I haven't experienced life with adolescents yet with all that that promises). Nowadays when other mothers say, as they sometimes do, 'How can you cope having your children at home all day?' I think that we have all had to cope with some degree of difficulty with our babies and toddlers: if you can do the hard part with the under-fives, then you can probably cope with the rest.

Although motherhood was not at all as I had imagined, I enjoyed it intensely. It was such a relief when the crying stopped that I was only too pleased to spend my time talking to Hosanna and playing with her. The experience of those early weeks probably helped me towards being more responsive and involved with her. When she was a couple of months old we moved from our graciously shabby attic flat across the city to a rented house with a small garden. Like practically all other mothers, I had the job of running the home. Like many others, doubtless, I disliked domesticity and derived little feeling of satisfaction from housework and cooking. Consequently I arranged my day so that I could feel that doing things with Hosanna was my main work and the household chores were fitted around it.

We noticed that Hosanna's development followed a cyclical pattern. She would have a burst of progress which might extend over several months and would usually manifest itself in many different areas of development at once. This might then be followed by what seemed to be a resting period or what might be a period of assimilation. Even now we can look back and clearly identify this pattern of plateaux and valleys in Hosanna's life.

The first had begun at five months. Hosanna made the transformation from a babe in arms to a young person determined to crawl, sit, stand, walk and climb, all as quickly as possible. She seemed to acquire new skills with every passing day. At ten months a period of comparative rest began. At twenty months her second period of acceleration came. Her language and comprehension improved so dramatically that it seemed quite magical to me. Overnight she was able to recognize and name ten different colours, for example, which took me by surprise. A further period of blooming came at two and a half. She could now draw people, insects and animals and would write rows of letters, so strong was her urge to write.

Quite early on, we got into what I called the toddler social whirl. We went to Mother-and-Toddler groups, to the story time at the library, to the community room at the local school. We went to the toy library and the dancing group. We went swimming or on outings with other mothers and their children. We spent a lot of time visiting or being visited. Swaps were arranged with several other women so that we mothers could have 'time off'. Victor started studying as a mature student on a degree course when Hosanna was two and I attended 'A' Level classes on a couple of afternoons a week. Those were quite busy days; Hosanna and I often seemed to be moving between one place and the next. It was all far from my original idea of a rural, almost isolated existence with the children learning within the home from the example of the adults around them.

Our way of life then was influenced by the fact that we lived in a city; and if you have to live in a city, Bath is one of the loveliest and most civilized. The circle of people I knew tended to be aware of what was going on – where there was an event for children or women, places where you could spend an afternoon with toddlers – so there was always plenty to do. Because Hosanna was as yet an only child and was by nature outgoing and sociable, I felt she needed very frequent contact with other children so I set about providing this.

In that period I did a lot of reading about childcare and discovered many parallels to my earlier ideas in the pages of works by Montessori and Rudolf Steiner. These two may seem like opposite ends of a spectrum but they each had a very clear and valid picture of quite different aspects of the nature of the child.

Montessori advocated early training of infants. She wrote of the serious approach of the very young to learning. Her idea was that there is a correct time of life – which can vary from child to child – when she will be ready to learn a new skill. In our experience this was borne out by Hosanna's cyclical pattern of development. Montessori believed, as I entirely agree, that adults endow children with many childish attributes by limiting their access to the wider world and by preventing them from doing things they could do perfectly well for themselves. What I did not agree with was her emphasis on the child's wish to work and her dismissive view of the less workmanlike features of childhood. In her writings she sometimes seemed to treat imagination as an undesirable childish trait. I had a daughter whose serious desire to work was coupled with a stronger desire to play – and I mean *play*. Play and imagination are essential elements not just of childhood but of life.

Rudolf Steiner's views on education were concerned less with the intellectual development of the child and more with her spiritual wholeness. He felt that parents should have a respect for the child's dream-time, which is something I firmly agree with: parents should guard against making everything educational and consequently damaging the child's sense of wonder. He believed that for the first seven years, while she still had her milk teeth, a child was like a sense organ, taking in all that went on around her. For this reason the parent had to be aware that she was an example for the child. I was drawn to this idea though I could not agree with his predetermined phases of childhood. For example, he maintained that it was detrimental to the child's well-being to be taught to read and write before they reached the age of seven. I disagreed. I felt it would be positively perverse not to help a child who is keenly interested in reading and writing – as both my daughters were from a young age.

If I learned nothing else from my early plans and those first years with Hosanna, I learned that life does not always run in accordance with theories, however convincingly right they seem. Neill, Montessori, Steiner and the other great educators have given us a fund of ideas to draw from. Rather than keep to any one system, we have tended to consider what works best for us as a family and to adapt as we go along.

2

The Five Hundred Days

When Hosanna was three, I went with her to look at several playgroups. I had recently read accounts of Montessori's *Casa dei Bambini* in Rome and Susan Isaacs's Malting House School in Cambridge, both of which were pioneering schools for the very young. With these examples in mind, I could see that some of my local playgroups looked pretty uninspiring.

We watched the organized singing games. We looked at the rows of identical spaghetti pictures or the masks which had been cut and glued by adult helpers. We did see some lively-looking groups with climbing frames, sand-pits and perhaps an open door in sunny weather but nothing ever seemed that impressive. I always had the feeling that I could do better in my own home. Somehow so many of the children at the playgroups we saw had an aimlessness about their creativity and play, in a few cases almost a bleakness, whereas children I saw in my own home and in the homes of the people I visited had a real sense of purpose and resolution in their actions.

We did track down a very good playgroup, though, run by a woman who was disenchanted with the usual church hall scene and so ran the playgroup in her own home. The group was limited to ten children only. Mothers were allowed and even encouraged to stay unlike at some of the other playgroups where they were instructed to leave their children at the door and to disregard any tears. There were two helpers, one permanently available to read stories and one to supervise but not organize art and crafts. There was no fixed routine to the morning. The children could drink their milk when they wanted to and be read to for as long as they wished. There was a garden with apple trees to climb, rabbits to pet and a kitchen for cooking and jelly-making. It seemed ideal so Hosanna was enrolled for two mornings a week.

At home Hosanna was learning to read so we were spending a lot of time looking at books together. We very quickly got to the situation where I was having to prize Hosanna away from a book to go to playgroup. On the way there she might want to stop to look at a snail trail shining in the sunlight or to examine moss growing on a wall. I was aware that these were things we should be lingering over and that I was having to hurry her away from what she was interested in, to get her to playgroup on time.

And when we got there, even there at this best of playgroups, I saw again that same aimlessness that I had seen before: children wandering up to an easel and doing a dib–dab with the paintbrush – not the beautiful, considered, colourful paintings they might do at home but the few strokes that a child might do simply because the paints were there and why *not* have a go? – then perhaps listening to the story for a while with half an ear before wandering off to see what else there was.

There was even a boy there with a blue blanket, like some archetypal child who can just about cope if he has his comforter with him at all times. He waited by the door for his mother to come and collect him, almost from the moment that she dropped him off in the mornings. He had been going to playgroup for two years and he still had not settled in, even at this small, gentle playgroup. He would be starting school the following term. I wondered how he would cope there. It was difficult to see the point of playgroup if it was not producing socially able, busy, interested children.

Hosanna missed quite a few days of playgroup that first term. This seemed to be the best way to deal with it – to use it when it seemed a positive benefit to go and to stay at home when life was more interesting there. What a pity playgroup – and school, too, for that matter – could not be a resource that you could use when you wanted to. It struck me that paints and playdough were much more interesting to a child when she had to ask for them and help get them out. When they were there, already set out as at playgroup day after day, was it quite the same thing?

After only one term the leader had to move to another town and so the playgroup, under a new leader, had to find new premises. Installed in a church hall, it rapidly changed its character. The number of children had to be increased to pay the rent. Gone were the pets and the activities like making butter or going to watch the men digging up the road. In came the set story time, milk time and organized singing time. The mothers were asked not to stay. The leader assured us that children had to get accustomed to playgroup because school was never far away and they had to get used to it sometime.

I wondered about that boy with the blue blanket. I now saw him every morning crying as his mother led him over the green to school. What had his time at playgroup done for him? School was clearly an ordeal. Hadn't playgroup just brought forward and extended that ordeal by two years?

I thought about this. Yes, school wasn't far away. I sat down and counted up the days until Hosanna would have to start school. I found that we had five hundred days left. I was shocked. Now that the days had been counted they no longer seemed infinite, as they had before. Each day was now precious. When I spoke to Victor about the feeling of loss that this gave me, he suggested that I should write about it, as a way of coming to terms with whatever decisions I made.

I decided to start a diary in which I would write every day about Hosanna and the various issues concerning her upbringing. I called my diary *The Five Hundred Days*. I numbered each day's entry. I started at day five hundred and worked down to zero. My hope was that by the end of the book I would have resolved the question of whether my original view of childcare was the right view for me or whether children really needed the system that adults had decided was best for them, a system that we were fast being drawn into.

As I noted in my first entry in the diary, sending Hosanna to school was like throwing in the towel completely on all hope of life as I would have it be. Yet it seemed almost inevitable that she would have to go to school. It seemed to me that my life needed to be transformed before I could contemplate her not going through the system like everyone else. Here I was living in the suburbs of Bath on a housing estate, almost directly opposite a school, living a life that often seemed to me bogged down by domesticity. How could I justify taking a giant step like not sending Hosanna to school in such circumstances? Surely I needed to be a person of extraordinary talents and gifts to consider doing such a thing? Surely we needed to be physically isolated so that Hosanna would not stand out as being the one girl in the street – in town! – not going to school? I could not see how I could consider doing such a thing when the life I was living was so mundane.

Eighteen days after the start of my diary I decided we would stop playgroup altogether. Hosanna was not enjoying it so it was pointless to continue. She became noticeably more independent almost straight away. She also made rapid strides in her reading although admittedly she may have been due for one of her inexplicable surges forward.

However, I still had a mental picture of the ideal nursery school as described by Montessori, Susan Isaacs and others. At that time virtually everything I read about the education of the under-fives pointed to the benefits of young children learning not at home but in groups with their peers, in well-equipped nursery schools. When Hosanna was four the school starting age was raised in our county so that the rising fives were no longer allowed to start school. This had resulted in a mass exodus from the playgroups into nursery schools – a sort of panic rush by mothers who felt that playgroups were not going to be enough to carry their children right through to five plus. Most of the children we knew suddenly disappeared into the one state school in Bath which had a nursery class or into various different types of private nursery schools. I was still concerned about giving her plenty of access to other children so I decided to have another look at the available alternatives. We went to see the nearest Rudolf Steiner school but it was too far away to consider seriously. There was a nursery school in town, reputedly run on Montessori lines, so I decided to give it a try and to send Hosanna for two days a week.

On the first morning she went in cheerfully and was immediately drawn in. She looked interested. When I went back to collect her she rushed out like a missile. In answer to my questions she said she enjoyed it and so I was pleased. But even on that first morning I noticed she was extraordinarily excitable, to the point of irritability.

All through lunch she chattered so incessantly and unnaturally that I felt a curious sensation of being out of touch with her, something I had never felt before. I had heard of mothers who said that, when their children started school, they suddenly felt a great gulf open up between them, as if they had become strangers. Most mothers learn to accept this. I felt perhaps this was just part of the natural process of separation, the gradual loosening of bonds that goes on from birth. Yet I knew it was not that my perception of her behaviour had changed. She had become exaggeratedly over-active after her morning, as if she needed to release some pent-up pressure. I wondered what had happened to cause such apparent tension. Although she chattered without pause, she did not want to talk much about her morning. This happened each time she came home. It took several hours to wear off.

After a few weeks, Hosanna began to complain about going. It was becoming clear that she was not enjoying it. A friend of mine was temporarily helping out at the nursery school. She asked me how successful I was finding it. When I hesitated before replying, she remarked that Hosanna looked, as she put it, glazed with boredom the whole time – as did several other children there. She thought this was not at all surprising. There was something too bland and plodding about it all, she said. Perhaps this accounted for Hosanna's behaviour when she came home.

One day, a week or two after that, I was telephoned by the teacher who asked me to come and collect Hosanna. She had evidently refused to sit down to 'work' when asked to and was now demanding to go home. On my arrival there, the teacher informed me that an incident had occurred in which Hosanna had not stopped playing with her friend when she was told that she must sit down and 'do lessons'. The teacher had given her, as she told me, 'only a light tap' and Hosanna, upset, had insisted upon going home. I was very surprised – not at Hosanna's behaviour but at the teacher's. Smacking a child of barely four as a way of encouraging her to learn seemed positively bizarre. It did not sound like a part of any Montessori system I had heard of.

Hosanna and her friend had meanwhile settled down to do some drawings which they were rapidly finishing off because they both wanted to come home. Hosanna finished and said, 'Shall I write my name on it?' All their drawings and other works were marked with their names by the teacher at this nursery school. As I was saying, 'Yes, go ahead', the teacher sprang forward to write for them. Seeing them both quickly write in their names for themselves, she drew back and said, 'Oh, I didn't realize they could write their names.'

All the four-year-olds, including Hosanna, were given tuition in writing by the teacher every day. Perhaps it was not odd that, in maybe a dozen of these lessons, the teacher had not yet realized that they could write something as basic as their own first names. To be fair to her, perhaps she had not had much success at getting them to sit down at all! But it did strike me as being a typical aspect of schools in general. This woman, I realized, had got to know very little about these children and what they could or could not do. Perhaps she had some system of teaching that she was working through and, as far as she was concerned, they could not do something until she had taught it.

It suddenly struck me that, if Hosanna were to go to school, this might well be the beginning of a whole series of incidents, from minor ones to others that might be far-reaching and serious. It was not that I felt that this teacher was particularly culpable – although I did not agree with her methods – but I felt that this was typical of what we might meet in future schools, an approach to education designed to put any child off altogether. Hosanna did not return to nursery school and I began to suspect that, however ideal it might seem from the outside, no school actually lived up to its promise.

At about the same time as this incident, I had two interesting conversations, both of them with mothers of children of about Hosanna's age – women I did not know very well but who often stopped to talk to me in the street or the park. The first had a four-year-old daughter. She had withdrawn her child from playgroup and had sent her full-time, five days a week, to a convent school.

She mentioned the length of the school day which she

admitted was rather over-long for a four-year-old. She said that her daughter came home very tired. However she assured me – and herself – that, when a child was overcome by tiredness and laid down her head on the school desk to try to sleep, the nuns – who were kindly people – would turn a blind eye and not haul the child back to work. I listened appalled. I was astonished that anyone should even consider this as kindliness. It seemed to me an outrage to young children. If a child of four was tired and wanted to sleep, a school desk to rest on was a pretty poor concession.

Naturally this made me wonder even more why we were sending our children to these nursery schools. Doubtless this mother felt her child was gaining some benefit from the extra year at full-time school though to me, as an outsider, it was difficult to see what it was. What possible benefit could outweigh this tired year lost in a classroom? And yet I had convinced myself that a couple of mornings a week might be good for Hosanna. Just like this other mother, I was trying to disregard the evidence that I could quite plainly see. I had dismissed it as part of some necessary adjustment.

The conversation with the second woman was like a breath of fresh air and just what I was ready for. She has since become a firm friend. She is a former teacher who has taught at both primary and secondary level. She said her experiences at school as a teacher had made her feel that school was no place for anyone, and particularly not for a young child. She had decided not to send her two children to school until they were at least seven. She had also decided not to bother with playgroup as that seemed to her just to combine some of the worst aspects of infant school. This idea had met with great disapproval from her friends and from her doctor and health visitor although her older child was only three. It struck me forcibly that we were living in a pretty strange society where four-year-olds were 'allowed' to rest on their desks and three-year-olds not going to playgroup caused disapproval. What on earth were we doing to childhood? The very things, like playgroup, that might have been originated to enrich children's lives were now being used to extend their years in the school system.

This mother had just joined a self-help organization for parents who supported the idea of education out of school. It was called Education Otherwise. Its name had been taken from the passage in Section 36 of the 1944 Education Act which states that a child must be educated by attendance at school – or otherwise. This was the perfect moment for me to meet such a person, just as I was turning back to my earlier rejection of schools. I had heard on the radio about the group Education Otherwise but I had missed getting their address. I also had a magazine clipping about them, again with no address, although this suggested, incorrectly, that they had organized classes run by parents rather like an alternative school network. But no, here was this mother intending to do exactly what I had wanted to do all along – simply continue to let her children learn in a normal home environment. Victor and I joined the group soon afterwards.

Up to this point I had thought that something radical like keeping children out of school could only be done in a situation where normal conditions did not apply. The Education Otherwise newsletters were clearly saying this was not so. There were actual advantages in having access to public transport, libraries, museums, clubs and classes if you wanted them – and, of course, other people. Until we were able to move to the country, we could get on with home education here in Bath. Most important of all, the main effect of hearing about Education Otherwise was that it made me realize that I would look back and regret it if I did not give home education a try.

The decision not to send Hosanna to school was now very easy to make. I could see that, just as the ideal school did not exist, I did not have to achieve some ideal state myself in order to continue educating her at home. I was more satisfied with what I had to offer my four-year-old than with anything a school seemed able to offer – and she certainly preferred it. I realized that this would continue to be so at five or six or seven – perhaps at any age.

Learning from the other mother's experiences of disapproval, I did not alert the welfare services in advance. I decided to lie low and say nothing until Hosanna actually reached official school age. When the health visitor called and asked which playgroup she was at, I said casually that really she needed something a little more interesting than playgroup so we were giving it a miss. The health visitor was quick to sympathize, saying playgroup was a waste of time for an intelligent child! She went away assuming I was just dying to get her into school so I did not bother to disillusion her.

Hosanna was then due for the pre-school check-up, a physical and mental assessment on which notes would be sent on to be included in her school records. I realized I would almost certainly be asked which school she was registered with. I went to the clinic prepared to tell them of my intentions but only if I was directly asked. To my great disappointment, when I arrived I found that the doctor taking the assessment clinic was one I knew well. I feared that, if I told him, he would just say something like 'Oh come now, don't be ridiculous. You can't do that' and I would have to argue my case with him, which would be more difficult than with a complete stranger. I had already privately nicknamed him Doctor Pangloss some years ago when he had pooh-poohed my arguments for a home birth. He had not actually said, 'All is for the best in this the best of all possible worlds' but I was always half expecting him to. I sat there wondering how I could avoid telling a lie without sounding too idiotically vague.

I was very relieved when, instead of asking me which school, he genially named the school across the green from me, taking it for granted that she would go there. 'It's so near to you,' he said, to which I quietly replied, 'It's just over the road'. 'Oh, lovely little school,' he said approvingly and promptly wrote it down. I was over that hurdle.

Victor had been sympathetic to the idea of home education from the beginning. I always knew that he would back me if I took the decision not to send Hosanna to school although I knew that, initially, it was my decision to make – following my star as he called it. In Hosanna's earliest years he had played a very active role as a parent. In the last year or so of his degree course – the time just before Hosanna was five – he was less able to be involved so all the help with reading, writing and early maths was done by me. Once his course was over, his involvement increased again although, perhaps from habit, at first I carried on with the bread and butter work, as I called it. The work he did with her tended to be in concentrated sessions, making things, experimenting, exploring ideas. He is particularly good at education through conversation: better than I am, I feel.

When I came to the decision that Hosanna would not have to go to school, Victor came up trumps. I had expected that he would agree but I thought he might have reservations. Or I thought he would agree but treat it as *my* decision – which would mean that, if it did not prove a success, it would be basically my failure. So I was greatly cheered when Victor, recalling his own bitter memories of school, declared himself strongly committed. Educating Hosanna at home had become a shared decision.

As the five hundred days of my journal drew to an end I was firmly confident about our decision. We were moving into a new more home-based phase. Hosanna and I returned to our old pattern of reading together for as long as wanted in the mornings, talking and going about our day in the way that suited us. The mother-and-child groups were no longer appropriate. Apart from playgroup, most things were aimed at children either older or younger than Hosanna – it seemed that school in some form, or preparation for it, took up all the energies of the rising fives and the five year olds. Besides, I no longer had that feeling that we always had to be doing something for her to be stimulated and socialized. I realized she was learning more from our perhaps seemingly unstructured days at home and that she was fully as out-going, confident, sociable and capable as any other child I saw.

Perhaps another reason for this shift of emphasis was the fact that I was now expecting my second child. This helped to confirm my feelings about home education. It would have seemed very odd to have spent so much energy and time on Hosanna only to put her on to some educational conveyer belt for general processing while I started all over again with a second child. It seemed right to educate the two children side by side. Hosanna would surely have a lot to offer the baby.

The baby would be an educational experience – if nothing else! – for Hosanna. There would not be that problem of Hosanna feeling excluded from the family circle, which I have observed happening in families where a baby is born shortly before or after the older child starts school.

It was a time of great affirmation. We came to the enterprise of home education aware that it was a great responsibility. It may not always have been easy but it has always been interesting and challenging. We are drawn on by the possibilities that are always opening up before us. It is a continuing adventure.

3

We Contact the L.E.A.

At Hosanna's fifth birthday party there were several children who were starting at the local primary school the following term. Their mothers had been invited to a meeting at the school and they were talking about it while waiting for their children at the party. There was quite an animated discussion going on. I was the only mother present whose child would not be starting school. That was the first time it had really struck me that we were already out of the system – Hosanna had not been registered, we alone had not been invited to any such meeting.

It made us realize that the time for informing the authorities of our intentions was drawing near. The legal requirement was that a child should start 'full-time' education in the term following her fifth birthday. Hosanna's birthday was in July so we decided to write to the Local Education Authority (the L.E.A.) during the summer holidays. Just before the start of the autumn term we sent off a letter to the Chief Education Officer to inform him that, 'after careful consideration', we had 'decided to take responsibility for the education of our daughter Hosanna, aged five, in accordance with our duty under Section 36 of the 1944 Education Act, otherwise than through attendance at school' (the wording suggested by Education Otherwise).

We then had to wait, not knowing at all what their response was going to be. We did not know of any other family in the county who were not sending their children to school and so we were unable to find out in advance what the L.E.A.'s policy on home education was. We had no idea what we were letting ourselves in for. In spite of this, it was quite an exhilarating time.

We knew that there were families in some areas who were educating their children at home quite happily without any opposition from the authorities. We could gather this much from the Education Otherwise newsletters. However, the

situation varied from county to county. We also knew of
families in other areas who were running into difficulties. In
some cases, they were being threatened with court action:
there were one or two legal battles going on. Later we were
even to hear of cases where families had to deal with the threat
of a Care Order – of having their children taken into care by
the local authorities – because of disputes over educational
matters.

We had to consider how we would respond if we ran into
difficulties and whether we would be prepared to go to court
over it. The last thing we wanted was a crusade, battling
against the authorities, but we felt we would fight if we had to
for what was our legal right.

We decided to co-operate where possible rather than to
confront the L.E.A. Whatever we thought about the
education system, we recognized that people working in it had
to believe that it was worthwhile. If we were heavily critical of
the system in our dealings with its representatives, we might
find ourselves with more of a fight on our hands. They might
interpret our criticism as an attack not just on school but also
on themselves, on their own way of life. If we could not expect
them to be in agreement with us, then at least we wanted them
to be objective. After all, we were not out to convert them. We
decided not to bother with 'school-bashing' but to put across
our own case, which was not so much anti-school as
pro-home education.

We could not see that they would have any grounds for legal
action against us. We may not have been sending Hosanna to
school but we *were* educating her. She could already read
fluently. Her writing and maths work was on a level with the
sort of thing she would be doing at school in the next year or
so. We put great emphasis on her being out of doors much of
the time – not cooped up doing formal work and it seemed to
us that we had the balance about right. They could not argue
she did too little work, because she was not lagging behind her
peers at all – and how could she be, since she was only just five?

Parents who educate their children at home often feel
pressure that their children must be seen to be above average in
everything. Of course, this is nonsense. Not all children at

school are above average or even up to average in every subject
– or even *any* subject. The L.E.A. can hardly demand
something of a home-educated child that they do not expect
from all their school-educated children.

This question of comparison is important. If it were to be
argued that all children benefit from school then we have to
consider not just the brightest in the class, or even the average,
but all the children down to the least clever, the least happy,
the least well-adjusted. It then becomes easy to see that home
education compares very favourably with school. It could not
do worse than the worst of school and school should not be
judged just by its successes.

So, even if they judged Hosanna's work by some supposed
average, they could not say she was doing too little work. Nor
could they argue that she did too much. At that time she
usually did less than an hour a day. We always made a point of
putting informal education first. If we wanted to go for a walk
along the canal and talk about locks or the role of the
waterways or wildlife – or nothing at all – we would do this
and drop any idea of work at home for the day. She was
sociable and happy. We could not see that it could be argued
that school would make her more so.

But it was rather nerve-wracking, not knowing at all what
the response to our letter was going to be. I imagined that
some official might call on us unannounced so we took care to
be up, dressed and looking tidy and organized early in the
morning. A day or two passed by and then a telephone call
came from a slightly uncertain-sounding man who said he was
an Education Welfare Officer. He asked, very politely,
whether he might come and visit us – when it would be not too
inconvenient for us.

I was very pleased at this initial approach. He gave me the
impression that he was not sure how to deal with us, as if no
procedure had been established for cases like ours. There was
always the possibility that he was coming to serve us with
notice of court proceedings while being terribly polite, but
this seemed unlikely. I could not imagine that a planned policy
of coercion would begin with such a tentative call.

Still, we felt quite nervous about his visit so we decided to appear as if we expected to sail through without any difficulties. We thought we would try to prevent him from playing the official with us, if possible, and so we decided to avoid anything that might seem like a formal interview. Victor and I agreed in advance that we would ask him into the kitchen rather than into the sitting room and to treat it as a perfectly everyday conversation. To us it was quite a momentous occasion – our first encounter with the L.E.A. – but we were determined to act as if it were simply a matter of course and we fully expected their support.

On the afternoon that he was due to come, we let Hosanna play in the garden with her friends as we did not want to make her feel self-conscious by having her in the room while she was being discussed. We decided that we would not allow her to be put through any testing of any sort, or at least certainly not at this stage. If this was requested, I was prepared to refuse, pointing out that a child of five, just starting school, would not be subjected to individual testing by a stranger and so it was not reasonable to ask it of Hosanna.

The Education Welfare Officer arrived, was duly invited into the kitchen and all went to plan. Hosanna popped in occasionally from the garden to put in the odd word. She found it all amusing and probably seemed very cheerful and out-going. He was friendly, interested and not at all threatening, to our great relief. He explained that his visit was merely to check out our circumstances – that we did not have her working at a treadmill in some family sweatshop, for example – and he very soon said it was clear that we were genuinely concerned about our daughter's well-being and education. He admitted that a case like ours was new ground for him. He usually deals with truancy cases.

The only times he had come across the question of home education, he said, was with one or two parents whose children were nearing school-leaving age and were perhaps in trouble of some sort, either with the school or the police. We said we felt that home education was just as valid whatever the circumstances and might be the best thing for a teenager in trouble but he clearly did not see it in this light. He seemed to feel that education at home was acceptable if it was a question of principle, as in our case, but that it should not be done as a solution to an actual problem. A pity, we thought.

He said he was not qualified to judge Hosanna's work but asked to see examples of the things she was doing and the books she could read. Having said that, when he looked at her work he indicated that, in his opinion, it was all more than satisfactory. He told us that the next stage was a visit from an Education Advisor, who would assess Hosanna's work and advise us. (So we were over another hurdle! Hurrah!) At that time we were in the process of arranging a move to rural Wales (although it later fell through, alas) and the rest of the visit was spent talking about the benefits of living in isolation – which touched a chord in him. It was something, he said, that he had always wanted to do himself.

Before he went, he asked if he might 'have just a word or two' with Hosanna. He clearly respected her right not to be put through any sort of grilling so we said he could. By this time she had come in with a train set which she proceeded to set up around the kitchen floor. She was now engrossed in making a loop-line around his feet. It seemed to us a good example of life as it should be for a child, with total concentration on a chosen activity. He asked her, very kindly, whether she had 'any dollies' – at which she looked suitably aghast and said, 'Dollies? Blistering barnacles! I've got some dolls but I like playing Tintin and Captain Haddock!'

We had an enormous sense of relief after this visit. We could hardly have wished for it to have been better. We were left feeling positive and confident, aware that we might so easily now be feeling vulnerable and in doubt. It appeared that, in the absence of a policy on home education, the L.E.A. were going to be reasonable.

A few weeks later, we received a telephone call from the secretary of the Primary Education Advisor. We would be visited, we were informed, on a date in early February. Fine, this was months away yet, though it happened to be exactly when our new baby was due. We let the appointment stand but we knew that it was possible that we would have to postpone it when the time came.

February came and our second daughter was born. I did not have a name ready for this baby, having waited for a dream

like the one that had given me the name Hosanna. We called
her Fiorin, the name of a genus of wild grass. During labour, I
had watched the wind moving on the long grass outside so the
name was particularly appropriate. We later discovered that
Fiorin also means 'the Fairy Folk', which greatly suits the fair,
curly-haired girl she soon grew into.

It took me a while to get a daily pattern worked out after the
birth. Although Fiorin did not cry as Hosanna had, she was
another wakeful baby, one who thrived on rather less sleep
than I needed. We decided to cancel the appointment with the
Education Advisor. We had waited over five months so we
might as well be visited at a time that was convenient for us. I
had been confined to bed with high blood pressure for a few
weeks before the birth and we felt we had had quite enough
visiting what with the doctor and the twice daily visits from
the midwives, two at a time, for over a month. The new baby
had totally altered the fabric of my day and we could not see
any point in pretending that it had not.

For a while now, Hosanna's education was mostly
conducted through conversations and her own self-directed
learning. We noticed, as we have noticed since during periods
with little or no formal work, that she continued to make
progress. I can remember her around the time of Fiorin's
birth, sitting on my bed composing her first poem.

When Victor telephoned to postpone the appointment, the
secretary's rather prickly response was that they had a hundred
and fifty thousand other school-age children in the county to
look after – not just *our* child. She was unable to fix a date for
another appointment as the Education Advisor was too busy.
This pleased us immensely: it was like a reprieve. We certainly
were not clamouring to be seen.

We heard no more until one evening in the following June. I
had just returned from a day out with the two children, so we
all happened to be positively smartly dressed and full of
vitality and enthusiasm. Just before we came in, Victor had
energetically cleared up so even the house was looking
uncharacteristically tidy. We were sitting eating our supper,
laughing and talking about our day, when there was a knock at
the door.

It was seven o'clock in the evening. To my astonishment the

caller introduced herself as the Primary Education advisor. In a flash all those other occasions when she could have turned up unexpected filed through my mind – mornings when I had been up all night with the baby and had decided to lie in a while, afternoons when I felt I could not move for unwashed laundry, moments when life seemed at its lowest ebb! There had been countless occasions when I could have squirmed in my shoes at being visited. It seemed there had hardly ever been a better moment since Fiorin had been born . . . so I opened wide the door and let her in.

If I was amazed at her coming unannounced at this time of the day, I was equally taken by surprise by her opening sentence – that we were breaking the law by not sending our daughter to school. Nearly a whole school year had gone by and then this – and out of the blue, too: if they thought we were breaking the law – although we were not – why on earth had they let a year go by without a word of disagreement with us? I thought I would not let my good mood be spoiled – there was nothing to be gained by getting angry or upset. Mentally, I made my first personal rule for such encounters: keep as cheerful as possible. So I cheerfully countered her opening statement by quoting the relevant section of the 1944 Education Act.

She asked how we could wish to deprive our daughter of the joy of creating alongside other children – as she saw it. How could I reply to that? I was determined not to be drawn into an argument so I asked whether she could truthfully say that all children continuously found school a joyously creative experience. The joys of school were soon dropped.

After a series of questions, or challenges as they seemed to us, she then asked our reasons for teaching Hosanna at home. I said I found this difficult to answer off the cuff but she insisted that I should give my reasons fully – at which I had to point out that when she was sitting eating her supper at seven o'clock in the evening she didn't have someone come in and demand that *she* gave reasons for her whole way of life. Did she? And she took my point.

It was a bit like being an Aunt Sally at a fair. One minute I was quietly getting on with my life. The next I was suddenly expected to be available for a bombardment. We were prepared to give the L.E.A. any information they needed to satisfy themselves that Hosanna was receiving a suitable education but we would not be available for arguments at all hours and without advance notice. She had chosen her moment to come, after all, so in a sense she had come prepared. It was only common courtesy that we should receive the same sort of consideration that the head of a school would expect. Surely, no head teacher would tolerate a visit without an appointment . . . and in the evening! Nor would they have to justify the very existence of their school.

I felt that anyone coming to see us who called herself an Education Advisor should not be interrogating us but should actually be giving us advice. So I decided to ask her a question or two that would draw her back into her role as advisor. I asked her about the level in mathematics expected of a child in school when she moves up from the infants school to the juniors. I did not need this piece of information; I simply wanted to ask her something to change the direction of the conversation. And back came the reply as quick as a flash – if I did not know *that*, what was I doing teaching my child at home!

We learned a lot from these first meetings with the L.E.A. If our first rule was to keep as cheerful as possible, our second was not to feel obliged to get drawn into arguments with them about the reasons or merits of home education. If we did not need to justify ourselves for exercising our legal rights on other matters, we need not feel on the defensive, as if we have to argue our way out of a corner, about our right to educate our children at home.

Our third rule was not to accept visits without a prior appointment. It is important to be mentally prepared – the person visiting is prepared and knows what the L.E.A. is planning to do. The family being visited may have no idea what procedure they are going to be put through and so should at least have the benefit of knowing beforehand when to expect a visit. After this occasion when we were called on without an appointment – another Education Welfare Officer came unannounced a year or two later – we explained, pleasantly but firmly, that we were just about to go out so it was not convenient to see him then. We said we would be pleased, however, to see him another day if he would like to make an appointment. This was readily accepted and caused no ill-feeling. We asked for several days notice before any visit.

Our fourth rule was never to ask an Education Advisor for advice! We were later able to modify this to not to ask for advice until it is offered. We had realized the importance of appearing – to the L.E.A. at least – as if we were totally confident about what we were doing. I would suspect that if you appear doubtful about education at home or unsure how to proceed, you might well find yourself facing much greater opposition from the L.E.A. than if you act with self-assurance. It seems a pity that you cannot be honest about your problems or doubts – and we all have problems or doubts even if we feel we are making a success of our children's upbringing – without leaving yourself open to unsympathetic judgement. If a question about the standards expected of children in schools could get such a response, I wonder what would have happened if, on that first visit, I had actually asked for advice about how to *teach* maths. And yet I should have been able to.

After the difficult beginning, our first meeting with the Primary Education Advisor quickly became less combative and more friendly. Hosanna took an instant liking to our visitor which helped things along considerably. As she was leaving, she asked us to send in a curriculum and a timetable. I said, smiling, that we would not supply a timetable – since we did not work to one, and did not intend to, it would be dishonest to pretend we did. We agreed to send her a curriculum as this could be a general statement about the way we view education and what we might do in the future.

We sent off more of a declaration of intent, outlining some of our major reasons for educating Hosanna at home. We gave an account of the kinds of activities she did and the things we thought we might do in the next six months or so. Our account was fairly detailed. We reasoned that a full file would make the L.E.A. less inclined to feel that further action was needed.

Hosanna had now come to the end of her first year of learning at home – officially. In practice it was a natural continuation of all the learning she had done in those important first five years – unofficially. We no longer felt like the lone family in the county with children out of school. Membership of Education Otherwise was growing both nationally and locally. In Bath alone there were now two other home-educating families and a year after that there were five, as well as a number of others with younger children who were not intending to send them to school.

Since our first visit from the Education Advisor we have had further visits at eighteen month intervals. The beginning of the relationship may have been rather intimidating for us but it soon became much more relaxed and friendly. The L.E.A. seems to have accepted that we are not likely to change our minds so we are no longer told about the delights and benefits of school. There is no testing or examination. The Advisor has asked Hosanna if she would like to read to her. She has talked to me and the children and looked at the work we have had ready to show her. She has made helpful suggestions and has been positively supportive in her comments. We feel that we have come through, as far as the L.E.A. are concerned. We believe that our policy of aiming for friendly co-operation with them – combined with a degree of firmness on our part – has helped us to avoid unnecessary confrontation along the way.

4

Our Reasons – Practical

Parents who choose to educate their children at home do so for a wide variety of reasons. Some are aware that they can teach their children more effectively than schools can and may aim to reach a higher standard more quickly. Others may reject the values they see as prevalent in schools and may wish to find alternative ways of preparing their children for life. Other parents may have spent years standing helplessly by as their children floundered or suffered in the school system before they came to the conclusion that they would have to do it themselves.

People who decide not to send their children to school do not all have the same view of education; nor will they all have the same objections to the school system. We as a family had many reasons for our decision. We were surprised when we counted through them just how many areas of life they touched on – and we are just one family. It made us realize that educating our children ourselves was an integral part of our view of life – of our philosophy.

Although these are our reasons, I am sure that we hold them in common with many other families who have decided on the same course.

Keeping Responsibility

The most obvious reason for home education was, for us, the wish to keep full responsibility for our children's upbringing. We had been responsible for their coming into the world and we could see no good reason for suddenly delegating this responsibility once they reached the age of five.

Hours at School

We thought the hours of schooling were too long. At the primary end of the scale, we could see the children of our friends coming home from school too limp with tiredness to do anything and too drained even to talk about their day. The picture looked just as bad for secondary school children whose school day was extended into the evenings with homework.

We began to wonder whether it was necessary. Did a child really need to spend the best part of every day, for a minimum of eleven years, at school? Whatever were the skills they needed and why did they take quite so long to acquire? If these skills could be learned outside school, would it really take so many hours or was schooling an inefficient method of acquiring them? If it could be done in less time, it seemed a great pity that children were spending their lives unnecessarily confined in a classroom. It seemed to us too great a waste of childhood to accept that it could not be done in any other way.

School as care-taker

Once we started considering the long hours, we began to wonder whether it was only education that was going on at school. The length of time spent in school suggested to us that it was really a form of childcare, keeping younger children out of the way of their parents and older children off the streets. Once I began to think of it in terms of children being looked after, I realized that, not only did I not *mind* looking after my own children, I positively enjoyed their company. I saw no reason to shunt them off to be cared for by someone else. This is not to say that good childcare should not exist. There is a need for it and school does provide this necessary service for parents, many of whom could not carry on their working lives without it. Many parents want schools. All the same, I felt we should recognize that there is this element of childcare. It should surely be a service that can be utilized by parents not something that is forced upon them.

Choice of care-taker

When considering a childminder, most parents would prefer someone who will be sympathetic to their particular children, someone with broadly the same attitudes. If an arrangement proved unsatisfactory, they might well start to look elsewhere. When it comes to school, however, parents and children usually have to put up with what they get.

I first became aware of this when Hosanna was younger. If she was going to be looked after, I made sure it was by someone she liked and who got on well with her – and someone whose ideas on bringing up children roughly coincided with my own. There was never any question of 'Oh, this woman's been to Teacher Training College for three years therefore she must be irreproachable'. If choice of care-taker was considered important before the age of five, I could not see why it should be left to chance after that age.

The socialization myth

When people express surprise on hearing that my children do not go to school they generally find it easy to accept that they still get an education. The thing that they find more difficult to understand is how they go through that process known as socialization. And yet here they are, clearly 'well-socialized' – confident, able to get on well with children of all ages and, most noticeable of all, able to talk to adults without the usual inhibitions that so many schoolchildren have.

We have all assumed that children need school in order to learn how to mix with other people. I certainly assumed when Hosanna was five or so that we would have to compensate for this lack of mixing by letting her go to lots of clubs and classes. We soon noticed, though, that Hosanna was well able to cope when meeting new groups of people, children or adults. She seemed, if anything, more socially able than many of her peers. We gradually realized that the sort of socialization that you get at school sets you up for school and not much else. In life you meet a number of different people in a variety of relationships. When a child does not have to adapt to the thirty children and one adult relationship of the classroom she is better able to cope with this multiplicity of relationships. It is not often in life that we as adults have to deal with people or situations as a member of a squad of thirty – unless we join the armed forces of course. Also, a child can be more open with adults if she has not had to learn the peculiarities of the child-teacher relationship. This belief in the socialization aspect of schooling – held by so many people to be one of its indisputable benefits – is one of its greatest delusions. We only need the socialization that schooling brings because we have schools.

School is not the real world

In a home environment, children see the interests and activities of the people around them. They are able to learn from these examples, to be drawn along, to follow the same or different pursuits with varying degrees of attention and diligence. We realized that our children had contact with adults – admittedly mostly Victor and myself – who were interested in a whole range of subjects. Of course I am not claiming that we had had specialized training in these subjects at college or university (neither have many primary schoolteachers) but we had the cheerful interest of non-professionals that enabled us to lead the way and also to learn, ourselves, along the path.

We felt that if our children were to go to school they would be taken from an ambience of genuine interest and put into the hands of the professional teachers whose business it was to inspire interest in children, year after year after year. However enlivened by her subject a teacher may be, she still has the restrictions of the school timetable and the problems of communicating her interest to a number of children in a limited time. The process of teaching itself detracts from her credibility. (She talks about history because she's the history teacher. Do the fourth formers believe she would choose to spend her time, given free choice, teaching them about the Tudors?) A most obvious example for us was the idea of taking a young reader from a house overflowing with books – where reading was considered so interesting that any spare moment was an opportunity to read – to a school where the enjoyment of reading would be encouraged by a young woman who would herself probably never be seen reading for her own pleasure.

Learning limited by curriculum

Professional teachers admittedly have some advantages. They know exactly what to expect of a certain age group and exactly what they will teach them. But this has its disadvantages, too. It also restricts the child's learning because the possibilities open are limited by the teachers' expectations of children's abilities. Parents are aware of this in the case of very bright children who are frequently seen to be held back in school but they may often not be aware that the limitations of schools affect a much wider band of children than just the very brightest.

I am told by a parent that a local junior school, for example, has a system in its library where children can only choose books to read that are of the 'correct' reading level. The books are colour coded so that the child knows which books she may choose from. If that is not limitation enough, all the books in the school library are selected, presumably with great care, because they are deemed suitable for just that age group covered by the school. In the past few weeks I have seen Hosanna take to bed with her on various occasions the complete works of Tennyson, the works of Blake, a book on Magritte, the Penguin translation of the Odyssey – all books written for adults not children. She did not choose such books because she is freakishly advanced or because we encouraged her to. She chose them because they are as freely available to her as *The Wind in the Willows*, *Black Beauty* or any other book we have in the house. They were not colour coded as being out of her range. Children are not only limited by the choice of books in the school library. Virtually every aspect of the curriculum is chosen as being what someone has decided is suitable for that age range. The child is limited by those choices.

Teacher expectation

The effect of teacher expectation has even more worrying implications as was shown by some very interesting research by the American psychologist, Robert Rosenthal. He worked first with experimental psychology students, looking at the way their expectations could influence their findings in experiments with rats. In one such experiment he divided the rats into two groups. He labelled one group as 'superior', pretending that they had been specially bred to perform more intelligently. The second group were labelled as 'dull', again allegedly as the result of special breeding. He then set the students to work testing the rats to check the animals' intelligence. Astonishingly, the students were able to confirm that the so-called intelligent group of rats performed better than the supposedly dull group. What is more, the students judged the 'superior' rats to be pleasant and likeable; they watched them more closely and handled them more than the 'dull' rats.

The experiment was then tried on teachers but this time using not rats but school children. The children were tested and their teachers were told that this would identify those children who were about to put on an intellectual spurt. A number of children, selected entirely at random, were picked out and this 'information' was given to the teachers. When Rosenthal went back to test the children over a two year period, he found that those children whose supposed intellectual spurt had been brought to the teachers' attention actually performed far better in intelligence tests than they had previously. In some cases the difference in performance was very dramatic. Rosenthal concluded that the teacher's increased expectation of a certain child's intelligence resulted in that child getting more sympathetic attention which in turn produced a significant improvement in that child's performance. The expectation worked as a self-fulfilling prophecy. He wrote a book about his findings and called it, appropriately enough, *Pygmalion in the Classroom*.

If we find it alarming that such an experiment could be done in an unsuspecting school so that a random selection of children actually gets preferential treatment, we must also consider what damage teacher expectation is doing all the time. It could be argued, I suppose, that teachers are not selecting children at random for their special attention but are somehow able, with their professional experience, to pick out the abler children when not distracted by bogus test results.

But surely, even if that were true, *all* children, not just the brightest, are entitled to special attention. If Rosenthal's experiments show that teachers nurture intelligence, they also show that other children, too, could perform better but are held back simply because their teachers do not expect much of them.

School as a game of chance

This may all seem like little more than a game of chance. If the teacher thinks your child is bright, her chances of flourishing at school increase. As if that is not bad enough, intelligence is not the only factor. The teacher may like – or take exception to – any number of things about your child. She may also like – or take exception to – any number of things about you, the parent. And, of course, to increase the element of chance, this varies from teacher to teacher.

The daughter of a friend of mine provides me with a good example of the way a child's perceived performance can vary greatly from one teacher to the next. At her first school this child was considered exceptional, very bright and particularly charming. The mother enjoyed a happy relationship with the teacher and received only good feed-back about her daughter's progress at school. After a change to another teacher, the mother attended the next parents' evening full of confidence. She was amazed to be told by the new teacher that her daughter was 'too sociable' and 'too busy fiddling about to get down to work'. There followed a whole list of general complaints about this same child's behaviour, so many that it seemed that the teacher was objecting to her very nature. The mother knew perfectly well that the new teacher did not approve of her as a mother either, disliking those same aspects of her and her daughter that the first teacher had so much liked.

She concluded that for the next year or more her child would be perceived in an unfavourable light and would probably perform accordingly. Within the school system the best she could hope for was a more sympathetic teacher in the future. It may seem particularly sad when a child thrives with one teacher and fails with the next, but even less fortunate is the child who will not thrive with any teacher at school – and there are any number of those languishing within the system. Unless they and their parents have confidence in their abilities, they may go through life accepting whatever labels are put on them at school.

Responsibility for learning

A child is most likely to learn when she takes on for herself the responsibility for learning. Schools deprive children of the opportunity to do this. The emphasis is often on teachers teaching, as if children's learning comes about as some sort of by-product of this activity. This is most obvious at secondary level where a child's week is spent passing from teacher to teacher, each teaching her own subject quite divorced from the rest of the curriculum – and divorced from the child's life, too. At home such a set-up would be highly undesirable, even if it were possible to arrange. While we at home may – or may not – set aside time for 'schoolwork', the division between education and life – or one subject and another – is not distinct. Learning is a natural process that should not be taken from the child. Children learning at home cannot be spoonfed (or force-fed) by their parents all the time. They learn that they have to do most of it themselves, particularly as they approach secondary school age. It is important not only that a child can work and find out information by herself, but also that she knows she is responsible for her own education. I am not just talking about having a say in the direction it takes, the equivalent of the choice between Art and Physics or History and Geography in the third form. I am talking about the realization that it's all down to *her*, the person doing the learning.

The educationist, Paulo Freire, teaching literacy to Brazilian adults, noted how quickly they could learn to read and write, contrary to expectations perhaps, when they felt that it was necessary to acquire these skills. We learn most easily when we are sufficiently interested or when we ourselves have made the decision that the skill is worth acquiring. As adults we are usually freer to make choices about what we learn. When children are taught, regardless of their interest or their ability to see the point in learning the darn thing anyway, the chances are that they will take in very little. I am not arguing that a child never needs to learn anything she does not want to – but a child who feels responsible for her own education is more likely to accept the rough with the smooth.

Responsibility for life

There is another aspect to this need for a feeling of personal involvement. School takes control of a young person's day and, in doing so, takes away responsibility from her for structuring her day and planning her life. In a situation such as we have in the 1980s, large numbers of school leavers are being turned out each year to find that there are no jobs for them. These young adults who have had their days mapped out for them by school for the past eleven years are suddenly given a new freedom, a freedom for which they have not been prepared. The majority of them will be ill-adapted to their new unstructured lives.

I have sometimes been asked, 'What about the future? How will home educated children be able to cope with the world and compete for jobs with young people who have been in the system all their lives?' This falsely assumes that children educated at home are kept away from the real world whereas I believe that it is the children at *school* who are cocooned, who are more likely to fall apart when the props of the school system are taken away.

Freedom from school day

Being free of the school day has many other, more immediately obvious benefits. As a mother of young children I am aware that I don't need to be waiting at the school gates every day at half past three. I don't have to plan my day, or week or year, around school hours or terms. We can do things at our own pace, go out when it suits us. We can visit museums and places of interest during their least busy periods, not their most busy.

On summer mornings when we pass the schoolchildren, they on their way to school, we on our way to the park, I never fail to feel that we have made the right choice. And on cold winter mornings too, when we are sitting by the fire talking or reading our books – perhaps after an early morning walk with the dog – we often look out at the sluggish trail of children going over to the school with a feeling approaching amazement.

Freedom from worries about school

Freedom from school has benefits for parents as well as for children. My children have not needed to worry about being bullied in the playground, falling behind the rest of the class, keeping in with the teacher or whatever, and I do not have to give it a thought either. I am released from concern about the various aspects of schools. I do not have to interpret morning stomach aches or recurring sore throats that disappear mysteriously after ten in the morning. I do not have to wait until the next parent-teacher evening to know how my child is getting on.

A major worry for parents with children in state schools has been the damage done by a policy of cuts in spending and the perceived fall in education standards. One way or another, we are all affected. However, for us as a family it is a political issue – one we feel strongly about. Our children are not directly affected by shortages of books and materials, large class sizes, delapidated buildings or disruption caused by industrial action by underpaid teachers.

Being in touch

I am sometimes asked how do I know how well my children are getting on. It could be asked how parents of schoolchildren know how well *they* are getting on. They may have to try and draw what information they can from brief reports or the annual parents' evening. They may get some idea of how well their children are doing comparatively – perhaps first in English, about average in maths or just about bottom in everything – but they often have very little idea what the child actually knows and understands. The teacher is not necessarily a good judge of this either. Being in touch with the child and knowing what she understands more than compensates for this lack of comparison with other children.

Why start school at five?

Parents are allowed and expected to educate their children until the magic age of five (some might say the hard bit!) then suddenly the 'experts' must take over. Why at five? The sheer arbitrariness of this age was accentuated for us by the way that, in the county where we live, the accepted school starting age kept changing each time there was a County Council election. When Hosanna was three, the rising fives were expected to start school. Then, as she neared this age, a change in the balance of power in the County Council meant that no child could start school until the term after she was five (except in only one or two schools where there was a special nursery class). This was a cost-cutting exercise and had nothing to do with the benefits or otherwise of education for the very young. As Hosanna reached five plus, another election meant that suddenly all children over the age of four were able to start school. Mothers were now positively encouraged to send their children for this extra year. It made us wonder: if the age could be altered to suit political whim, or, more exactly, to suit financial theories, was the well-being of the children being considered at all? How could we really now be convinced that any particular age was the right age?

The parent is the expert

When the child reaches five, the local authorities are required by law to satisfy themselves that education is taking place. So, herd the children together, call it school and tell the parents that their skills are now not good enough. Call in the experts. In modern society this calling in of experts continually undermines the confidence of the individual. We are constantly being fed the idea that in many areas of life there are specially-trained people who know more about what we are doing than we do. I think parents are particularly susceptible to the loss of confidence that this can bring about. As Professor A.H. Halsey observed in the 1972 Reith Lecture, 'Fathers, and more especially mothers, inhabit a world which takes away their control and simultaneously insists on their responsibility for the fate of their children. . . . They are increasingly made to feel amateurs in a difficult professional world.'

If you have been close to your child for the first five years and feel that you understand her needs and abilities, then you may well be right – *you* are the expert on your own child. You may not have been trained in generalized teaching methods but what you know about your particular child must surely compensate for this supposed lack. A teacher cannot really be expected to be aware of the individual needs – the strengths, weaknesses, interests and abilities – of each of her thirty or more pupils.

The idea of every subject having its experts was brought home to me when I was asked to take part in a television studio discussion about education at home. The Programme Controller told me they had not yet arranged who else would be on the panel but he said they would try and get 'someone from the University – an expert on home education'! I wonder how anyone gets to be an expert on home education by being at a university. The implication, of course, is that a mere mother, a home educator for several years, still has to be off-set by *anyone* who can be labelled an expert.

5

Our Reasons – Political

School perpetuates inequality

As soon as we started to consider our reasons for not sending
Hosanna to school, we realized that some of our strongest
beliefs about society were being clarified in the process. It does
not take much examination to realize that school is an efficient
method of keeping things exactly the way they are.

The 1944 Education Act aimed to give a greater chance of
equality to all, but even in the days of expansion in the 1960s
the Robbins Report noted that the proportion of working class
boys at university was no higher than it had been in the late
1930s. Can anyone claim that things are getting any better?

Our country is still run, by and large, by people who were
educated at fee-paying schools. (For an obvious example, look
up the Cabinet Ministers and Government Law Officers in
Dod's *Parliamentary Yearbook*. In 1985 the overwhelming
majority were educated privately: 21 out of 26.) A leading
public school, Westminster, sends about 80 pupils to
Oxbridge each year. How many does your local comprehensive manage?

A myth has been allowed to flourish which suggests that the
imbalance in intelligence – or apparent intelligence – between
the social classes is created in the home and is levelled out at
school, that school gives children from underprivileged
backgrounds the help and stimulation that they would
otherwise be denied. I agree that intelligence is largely decided
in the home but school also plays its part in creating and
maintaining the imbalance. It is very important that school is
not mistakenly accepted in its benign role; it is not a gateway
to the world for all on equal terms. We do our children great
injustice if we do not recognize that schools not only hold
many children back but also that it is part of the system that
they should do so.

Even for those within the state-maintained part of the

system, the majority of children, there is a lack of equality of opportunity. For some unknown reason we seem to have accepted that brighter children need better facilities, more equipment, a higher staff-pupil ratio and better qualified teachers. Formerly these resources were concentrated in grammar schools. Nowadays, in an apparently more egalitarian system, they are often concentrated in the upper streams of the comprehensive schools. There is not, frankly, a great deal of difference except the gap is no longer so visible.

Social class – as well as intelligence – influences the quality of education on offer. In his book, *The Home and the School*, Professor Douglas observed that children from middle class homes (to use his term) had several times the chance of working class children of gaining grammar school places – even if they had had the same I.Q. at age seven. So in four years of junior schooling something had happened to cause working class children to do less well comparatively. We must ask ourselves to what extent schools are offering equal opportunity and to what extent they are helping to perpetuate the inequalities inherent in our society.

Professor Douglas found that in junior schools where there was a system of streaming, children in the upper streams improved their scores in tests while scores for children in the lower streams fell. The deterioration was greatest for the brightest children in those lower streams. He noted that working class children were more likely to be put into lower streams and middle class children into higher streams – even by junior school age. His findings can be considered alongside Colette Chiland's studies in France. She also found that, after five years of schooling, children's performances in I.Q. tests improved or deteriorated according to their social class.

J.W.B. Douglas went on to say that transfer between streams was very rare and suggested that this was because 'once allocated, the children take on the characteristics expected of them and the forecasts of ability made at the point of streaming are to this extent self-fulfilling.' It sounds like Rosenthal and his rats all over again.

It could be argued, perhaps, that things are better now that the 11-Plus Examination and grammar schools have largely disappeared. However, he noted that in areas of the country where the 11-Plus was dropped, the proportion of working class children gaining grammar school places *fell* and he concluded that selection based on interviews and teachers' assessments can be influenced more heavily by the social bias of those doing the selecting.

I am not suggesting that the 11-Plus was a fair system. I still remember the experience of being at junior school and being told the alarming fact that there would come a day when we had to come to school, when everyone else had a holiday, and we would have to sit a very important exam which would decide our future, all by ourselves, with no help from anyone, in an empty school. I can still see the deserted classrooms and unoccupied desks through my ten-year-old eyes. We were told nothing of what we might be asked to do in the exam. There was no priming or preparation at all that I was aware of. Practically all the children in my class failed, which was taken to be perfectly normal.

When I went to grammar school I was put between two girls who had been to fee-paying junior schools in the suburbs of North-West London. They talked about all the preparation they had been put through in order to pass the 11-Plus – the weekly tests, the drills, being told what sort of thing to expect – and both remarked that most of the children in their classes had passed. Even at the age of eleven it was clear to me that the children at my junior school had been hobbled when they had been entered for the race. My junior school was in Shoreditch, East London.

There is a further development as a result of cuts in education spending. A *Panorama* programme (shown on B.B.C. Television in March 1986) put forward the argument that we now have a three-tier system in operation in our secondary schools. As before, we have fee-paying schools on the top tier. It suggested that we now have a wide gap between schools in wealthier areas and those in poorer areas.

The programme showed three schools. The private school was well-equipped and morale was clearly very high. The pupils themselves expressed how fortunate they were compared to pupils at state schools. Business is booming for the private sector. In 1985 there was a 20% increase in applications for places.

A state school in a well-off area represented the second tier. The headmaster had actively encouraged parents to contribute towards their children's education through a system of covenants. When tax-paying parents agree to give gifts of money regularly to the school, additional money can be claimed from the Inland Revenue – the tax originally paid by the parents on their earnings. Aware that there is a crisis in schools' funding, many parents were glad to oblige.

The secondary school representing the third tier was in an area of high unemployment. Not only was there less money around generally, but also, with fewer tax-paying parents, a system of covenants was inappropriate. This school had to make do without any extra income. The difference was immediately apparent – unpainted buildings in poor repair and only half the money to spend on books and equipment that the other state school had.

So, in a system which is supposed to offer equal opportunity to all, we have poorer children being channelled not only into lower streams with the opportunity to become less intelligent, comparatively, than they were before they started school but also into poorly-equipped, under-funded schools. It is hardly surprising that so many fail to earn the badges of success – the examination passes, the university places, the worthwhile, interesting, well-paid and respected jobs. It seems to me that the system ensures not just that people from better-off backgrounds fare better in life, but also that this takes on the appearance of being justified. They come through school better qualified, apparently more intelligent. In my more jaundiced moments, this process of justification seems to me to be one of the major functions of school.

To return to those Cabinet Ministers I mentioned earlier, what sort of education do they choose for their offspring? Why, private of course. According to the *Guardian* (17th May 1986) only *one* senior minister apparently has enough faith in state secondary schools to choose them for his own children.

School makes children responsible for their own failure

Talking about British schools may make it sound as if all this is peculiar to our country with its deeply entrenched social divisions. Far from it. It is a global problem. Ivan Illich's book *Deschooling Society* outlines powerful arguments against school and focuses on Latin America where education plays a more obvious role in labelling children: the wealthy succeed while the poorer children accept their failure as being the result of their own lack of industry and intelligence. It seems that everywhere large numbers of children are being classified as failures by a school system designed to maintain the status quo. As long as a few very bright children can be seen to be reaping the benefits of a free education system we are assured that all is well, that opportunities are there for those who work hard enough, are clever enough and so on.

Now that the numbers of children at school are falling – when we could give all our children the education they deserve in smaller classes – there have been cuts in the numbers of teachers, teacher training places, places in universities, polytechnics and colleges, an effective erosion of teachers' salaries and students' grants as well as general cuts in expenditure on books and equipment. Those who make the decisions in this country clearly do not wish to expand educational opportunities.

A woman came up to me in a shop the other day and told me a very disturbing story about her son's school career. She remarked with understandable bitterness that school was only designed to benefit the small proportion of children who end up with academic qualifications. For the rest of them, she said, it served no earthly purpose but to mark them down as failures, as foil for the successful few. I was quite astonished. It was not what I expected to hear when I went out shopping, from someone who had never spoken to me before. The woman who had reached this radical conclusion was a caring mother who had witnessed her son being written off by a succession of teachers as being 'nice but dull', put into remedial classes and referred to schools for the subnormal or maladjusted. Her cheerful, bright five-year-old had become an unhappy and frustrated eleven-year-old. Fortunately for her and her son, her story had what could be seen as a happy ending. After a long struggle on her part, her son was discovered by an independent psychologist to be highly intelligent but to have learning difficulties. He was now at a boarding school, getting help and attention to overcome his problems. The mother was clearly pleased about this but commented that she had in effect lost her son as he was now away most of the time – not quite the happy ending it might at first appear to be.

Sadly, not all children are of above average intelligence. For every child like him who is fortunate enough to be plucked out of the remedial classes and have his abilities recognized, there must be thousands of others for whom there is no other place within the school system. At about the same time as I had this conversation, I also had a telephone call from a mother whose fourteen-year-old son was doing so badly in his remedial class that she felt that her only alternative was to remove him from school and teach him herself. She thought that she could not do worse than the school. She was becoming worried about his ability to communicate and was under the impression that he was never even encouraged to *speak* in school. I have had similar telephone calls before, and since. I cannot see how these children could fare worse at home with a caring parent than they do in school. Bright or dull, they do not deserve the generally poor treatment they are getting. For these children education is not an opportunity but a straitjacket, with the probability of a label of failure around their necks for life. And society generally will see that failure as being justified.

Returning to the matter of schools only being of benefit to those who are going to pass exams, I wonder if people realize that, at 'A' Level, the system is tailored to let only a percentage through. If in one particular year many students excel at a certain subject, they are not all awarded the high grades they deserve. The current guidelines about 'A' Levels given to the examining boards by the Government in 1960 specify that the top 10% of students in each examination should be awarded Grade A, the next 15% grade B and so on so that 70% of the candidates should pass with grades A to E. Sounds fair enough, I suppose – but it makes it clear there is no point in everyone doing well; 30% are still going to fail however good a performance they put in!

The very real cut-backs in higher education places mean that higher grades are being asked of today's candidates. In the 1960s it was accepted that any well-motivated school-leaver with any two 'A' Levels could get a place in higher education. Competition is now fiercer. Better qualifications are needed not just for places at university but at every level in the job market. A greater proportion of young people are effectively being labelled as not up to standard. In times of high unemployment, the blame for joblessness can be shifted onto the individual.

If you find the idea acceptable that the finishing post should be moved so that a certain percentage are guaranteed not to finish the race, you should also consider the significance of the fact that the distribution of grades varies from one examining board to another. There is no mechanism for comparing the standards of the nine G.C.E. boards. The Secondary Examinations Council (formerly the Schools Council) monitors each board's performance but comparability exercises are voluntary and occasional.

In 1983 the Associated Examining Board (A.E.B.) awarded grade As at 'A' Level to a far smaller proportion of its candidates than other boards. In four subjects only 1% or 2% got a grade A (all figures from the *Guardian* August 28th 1984). In the same year in some subjects the Oxford and Cambridge Board awarded grade As to over a fifth of its entrants. (Compare Oxford and Cambridge giving 22.2% of its entrants grade A in maths with the A.E.B.'s 5.3%, or 14.6% in economics with A.E.B.'s 1.3%). We might wonder how such a gap can exist. With no mechanism of comparison between boards it cannot be argued that the Oxford and Cambridge Board had better entrants.

The new G.C.S.E. examinations for 16-year-olds were intended to do away with the distinction between G.C.E.s and C.S.E.s. It has been widely reported that this will remove the idea of 'failure' since there will no longer be a fail grade. Of course it will only be a matter of time before we see which grades are *seen* as failure – by the school students themselves, their teachers, parents and would-be employers. In the *General Introduction* to the G.C.S.E. examination issued by the Department of Education and Science I find that the standard of the top grades, A–C, will be the responsibility of the G.C.E. boards and the lower grades, D–G, will be under the control of the C.S.E. boards! Does anything really ever change?

People generally accept that some children do not do as well as others because they are not as clever or as hard-working. The success or failure seems justified. But when you start looking at the education system more closely, you see that individual merit is not the only factor – yet that is the basis on which we accept the labels put on our children.

School Files

Many people feel uncomfortable at the idea that there are files kept on them to which access is denied to them but allowed to others. They have no way of knowing whether the information kept is true or false. It is equally disturbing to think that files are kept on little children which can influence their future education and employment prospects. Parents are not allowed either to contribute to these files or inspect them for accuracy.

School files often contain comments about the pupil's family and social circumstances, her personality and behaviour – as perceived by individual teachers – and predictions about her future prospects and potential. The Advisory Centre for Education (A.C.E.) and others have campaigned for many years for an end to secrecy in school files. (See A.C.E.'s information sheet, *1984: Time to End Secrecy*, for the argument for open records.) They have come across many examples where conjecture has been included in these reports. Some L.E.A.s have standardized cards with lists of categories; for teachers to tick as appropriate – in their opinion.

Certain information has to be kept about medical details and educational attainment. But files can be filled with all manner of pseudo-psychological misinformation parading as fact. Besides, as John Holt wrote in *Teach Your Own*, 'It is nobody's proper business that a certain child got a certain grade in a certain course when she or he was eight years old'.

The keeping of secret files, the contents of which may be disclosed to outside parties – even the Police in some cases – without being shown to the parents or the student herself, shows how in these days when parental involvement is widely acknowledged as one of the most influential factors in a child's education, it is only a token acknowledgement where schools are concerned.

School as a tool of social control

We may look at Russia or China and perceive that their schools have a function not just to educate children but also to influence their behaviour and thinking as adults. We may or may not realize the indoctrination that goes on in our own schools. Our view of history is an obvious example. Less obvious is the way in which our society's mores are, often quite unconsciously, impressed into a child's mind. We may welcome this kind of moulding – since it is inevitable that some values will be implanted. However, we should be aware that not just our children's but our whole society's future will depend on these values and beliefs.

Some parents may be blithely unconcerned about the way our children's schooling may be used to shape the future but our Government is very much aware. And very aware too, of the possibilities it offers for social control. To take one sinister example, an official Department of Education and Science memo, reported in the *Guardian* (20th August 1985), states:

> There has to be selection, because we are beginning to create aspirations which society cannot match. . . . If we have a highly educated and highly idle population we may possibly anticipate more serious social conflict. *People must be educated once more to know their place.* (My italics)

School limits our idea of education

I have heard a retired headmaster comment on television that learning is a three way process involving the child, the teacher and the parent. Now this sounds all very fine – even quite a concession. Until comparatively recently many teachers would not have included the possibility of the parent being in the picture. But, really, learning is not a three-way process at all – it is a process that goes on within the individual. A learner may draw from many sources. She should not be made to feel that learning is something in which teachers, or parents, have to play a role. A facilitator or guide or giver of information may well be needed at times, but we should get away from the idea that this headmaster was trying to perpetuate, which is that learning cannot go on without teachers.

As things stand, many children – and many adults too – see education and school as inseparable with the consequence that, when they leave school, they want to put it all behind them. We should see education as being life-long, as going on all the time, and not something we can turn our backs on gratefully when we leave the school gates for the last time. The link between school and learning is forged from our earliest days. Children are sometimes unwilling to read or write or do anything that vaguely smacks of school once they start going whereas perhaps only a few months earlier they were eager and interested to learn.

Education must be separated from the institution of school. Our perception of education has been impoverished because we see it as what goes on in school rather than what goes on in life.

Schools are unfair to girls

As the mother of two daughters, I find the recent studies on girls in schools alarming. It has been estimated that boys get 70% of teacher attention in mixed classes. When individual teachers have tried to redress the balance a little and spend half the time attending to the girls in the class, the boys became so disruptive that they forced the teachers' attentions back to themselves. Yet girls are widely accepted to be more able communicators from infancy on, generally speaking earlier and more fluently than boys.

It has long been accepted that girls perform better than boys academically throughout the primary years. In the days of the 11-Plus, the results had to be 'adjusted' in the boys' favour to prevent too many girls from being seen to be cleverer. It wouldn't do to have more girls getting the privileged grammar school places with all the advantages that that would have brought! But it was believed that, in secondary schools, girls failed to live up to their earlier promise and that boys caught up and overtook them during the teens – which made it seem acceptable that so many more boys went on to higher education. However in 1985 girls leaving school were better qualified than boys. (Of school leavers at 18, 18.5% of girls had one or more 'A' Level passes compared to 17.9% of boys. Of school leavers at 16, 14% of the boys left with no exam passes at all compared with 10.3% of girls.) So now we can see that right through schooling, primary and secondary, even with less than their share of attention from the teachers, girls tend to turn in better academic performances than boys.

However, the girls' academic advantage still does not help them into higher education or better-paid jobs, as the Equal Opportunities Commission points out. Girls tend to turn away from higher education into low-paid work. It is suggested that one of the reasons for this is the choice of subjects studied by girls. At 'A' Level 70% of passes in maths go to boys. In technical drawing 97% of the passes go to boys and in physics 79%. The proportion of girls taking up computer sciences has dropped over a five-year period: boys outnumber girls by four to one.

One of the hidden consequences of the current cuts in higher education is that more places that would have been available to young women are being lost. If girls tend to opt for the arts, social sciences and teacher training and these are the places being cut, then girls are being affected by the cutbacks to a greater extent.

In mixed schools, girls are more likely to perceive maths and sciences as 'male' subjects, particularly when taught by men, and to turn away to suitably 'female' subjects. It is hardly surprising that girls account for only 10% of all entries to study technical subjects in higher education. (The above figures come from the *Guardian*, January 28th, 1986.) H.M. Inspectors have recognized that the problem is so great that they have recommended that girls should be given separate science teaching. It has been noted that girls who were taught maths in single sex classes for the first two years of secondary school perform significantly better than girls of the same ability taught with boys.

Pat Mahony in her book *Schools for the Boys?* points out that there is another reason why girls do not do so well in mixed schools – harassment by boys. She observes that boys in mixed secondary schools spend time and energy trying to control and dominate the girls, while pretending to ignore them. She comments that in mixed playgrounds boys take up space with their games so that girls are forced into small groups around the periphery. In the classrooms, too, boys tend to spread themselves out, often physically leaning over the girls. In class, boys often heave sighs, groan or put down their pens in a gesture of exasperation whenever girls ask or answer questions. Teachers confirm that girls contribute less to lessons in the company of boys. And yet the girls note that away from school, away from the herd, individual boys act towards them perfectly normally. We should not just dismiss all this as 'natural' or 'biologically determined'. The fact that the boys do not behave that way out of school when they are away from other boys suggests that it is a consequence of pack behaviour, something that boys seem particularly prone to and which school provides a setting for.

Girls generally fare better academically in single sex schools but many parents dislike the idea of the sexes being taught in isolation from each other. Besides, most primary schools are co-educational and perhaps by the age of eleven girls have already received a good grounding in the submissive role. But it is not just in mixed schools that girls are going to encounter treatment that may encourage them to underachieve. Of teachers questioned in a recent poll, 42.3% thought that a woman's career was not as important as a man's. That does not mean, of course, that the other 57.7% thought that it was more important! If we entrust our daughters' education to teachers who undervalue their future, how can we expect them to value themselves?

In my experience, home educated children mix naturally with girls and boys, even if they do not have siblings of the opposite sex. Perhaps this is because they have had less exposure to the cliques and groups that are a feature of schools, the idea that certain people are all right to play with – or hang around with – whereas others are not. They are less likely to be subjected to constant pressure from their peers to behave in a particular way that is considered acceptable. I believe home educated children are more likely to deal with people as individuals and so there is less likelihood of their falling into single-sex groups and roles.

Sexual stereotyping is not just confined to schools, of course. It is a very rare parent who manages to eradicate it in the home. But you may wish to *try*. I certainly aim to give my daughters the fullest confidence in their abilities. They will need a firm base to enable them to cope with all the injustices they will meet outside the home.

Schools unfair to boys

I am sure that if I had sons I would be more aware of the way schools operate to the detriment of boys. I know several people who teach their children at home who feel that boys fare worse in schools than girls do. I have not heard the argument that they are held back academically but rather that they have to pay a high price to keep their place in the pecking order. While sexual stereotyping causes girls to take a back seat, it also forces boys into having to prove their masculinity or be subjected to ridicule.

Judging by the Education Otherwise newsletters, bullying is a not infrequent reason for adolescent boys to be taken out of school. 'Fighting' is often accepted as being a normal part of boys' lives, but when cases of bullying have been excessive enough to be recognized by the school, it is often the victim who is seen as the candidate for sessions with an educational psychologist – as if being beaten up by a gang, for example, is a sign of a character fault.

Anxieties have recently been expressed about the general level of playground violence by teachers of even the youngest children. It is suggested that this is the result of watching too much violence on television. While I quite believe things may have got worse as a result of television, the problem has always been there – Tom Brown's attackers were not inspired by any American T.V. series. Violence in schools is a product of any system in which large numbers of children are herded together, regardless of their lack of feeling for each other. Children need to be free to respond to each other as individuals, not forced into the company, day in day out, of a very large group of people with whom they may have very little in common. The set-up encourages the disintegration into mutually exclusive groups, invites a pecking order to be established and breeds intolerance which is then perpetually being carried out into society.

6

Our Reasons – Poetical

Loss of Bloom

I have heard that even teachers say you can tell the difference between children in the first class at infant school and those that have been there a year or two just by the look of their faces. They start off looking bright and interested but, within a few years, their expressions are already dulled. They lose their curiosity and with it their eagerness to learn. Teaching methods are devised to try to make learning seem more like a game but, even if the teachers are fooled, the children are not so easily taken in. What real game would you play week in, week out, according to someone else's rules and always at someone else's bidding, whether you felt like it or not?

There is a difference between the children we know who go to school and the ones who do not but it is hard to define exactly what it is. I am not alone in noticing it. Many people have remarked on it to me – people from whom I would never have expected such an observation. I am sure most people receive compliments about their offspring but I have noticed that, when people say to me that Hosanna or Fiorin have an uncommon 'niceness', they often comment that perhaps this has something to do with never having been to school. I am surprised, if school is universally accepted as being the best possible place for children, that so many people – quite ordinary people – make the link between the process of schooling and the loss of some of the 'niceness'.

I am not just being a fond mamma – I notice it myself of other people's home educated children. They are not blasé about the world, tend not to be 'Oh I know, seen it all before' like some of the schoolchildren we know. I have the impression that children at school are subjected to constant pressure from their peers not to appear stupid or naïve. Some of them develop the defence mechanism of trying not to appear too interested in anything they are told because it might show that they did not already know it or they fear it might make them look too gullible. Perhaps the pressure also comes from teachers, some of whom make a practice of setting up one child for general derision, encouraging children to score off each other.

Schoolchildren are under pressure to conform to the values of the group. In contrast, children who do not go to school are more likely to have the freedom to decide if they want to conform or not. Not being constantly subjected to group opinion allows them to develop their own views and values and to stick to them in the face of opposition. They are less likely to be forced onto the periphery of a group they might never really fit in with anyway. If they cannot be accepted for being what they are, then they can find friends who are more congenial. I notice my daughters are able to move between different groups of children with ease. I am sure that not going to school is part of the reason for this. They are not outsiders. I suspect that in a situation where children are herded together regardless of compatibility, there are always outsiders. Look in any playground at playtime – you can often see straight away those who constitute the groups and those who are excluded.

I think that children who are not forced into the constant company of their peer group develop a stronger ability to think 'No, I won't do that just because you are doing it' – which I am hoping will come in useful when my children reach adolescence. A recent report by the National Association of Head Teachers suggests that drug-taking among the young is now widespread, in wealthy areas as well as poor, and extends even down to eight or nine year olds. The Birmingham Advisory Committee on Solvent Abuse has become accustomed to dealing with cases of glue-sniffing among junior school age children. I am not suggesting that this only goes on in schools. I am suggesting that, in schools, children learn to conform to the code of the crowd.

Children need confidence in themselves, whether about their individuality or their abilities. In Pat Ashton's Aims of Primary Education Project of the 1960s, primary teachers rated 'self-confidence' eighteenth in the order of aims, one place behind 'obedience'. Secondary school teachers valued it even less, placing it thirtieth, while 'obedience' was placed ninth. In an article in the *Times Educational Supplement* (18th October 1985), a headmaster, Michael Sullivan, suggests that schools deliberately suppress children's confidence:

> Self confidence is developed through the reduction of fear, stress, uncertainty, confusion and failure – the very tools that too many of us skilfully use in the management of children in our charge. Children are fearful of verbal abuse, physical abuse and sarcasm. Children are stressed on the rack of tests and quizzes, often facing inevitable personal humiliation. They are confused by our bad teaching and then made to feel guilty by us for our own shortcomings as teachers. Children's noses are constantly rubbed in their failures; research repeatedly shows that we teachers are more lavish with corrosive criticism than constructive praise.
>
> Self-confidence is built out of self-respect and self-image. The images that schools create and reflect to their pupils are often distorted and flawed to satisfy the needs of the school rather than the needs of the children.
>
> Most children start school as enthusiastic, curious, active and imaginative beings. Too often our school system deliberately stamps out these sparks of vitality. Confident people are more challenging than predictable, passive, dull-eyed conformists. In an increasingly demanding and challenging world our children will need to be able to swim with confidence in a sea of uncertainty.

He suggests that any teacher wishing to nurture confidence will probably have to do so in the face of opposition from colleagues who are unlikely to welcome anything that challenges the traditional methods of control that govern most schools.

In contrast, the children we know who do not go to school have a special sort of liveliness and receptivity. The only way I can describe it is that they are more like *real* children – children who have not had a truncated childhood and who are not constantly looking over their shoulder to see if anyone has noticed that they have let their guard down for a moment.

This is what I think people mean when they speak of the 'noticeable difference', the 'niceness'. Perhaps this was what was meant when people said to Joy Baker, author of *Children in Chancery*, mother of seven children who stayed at home, that her children had an appearance of 'innocence'. I am not saying that no schoolchild has this special quality but that it is more evident among those who have not been through school. This does not mean to say that home educated children are in any way young for their age – combined with this real–child–ness is often a greater degree of maturity and a *lack* of childishness.

The needs of the individual

At home children can learn at their own pace and interests can be followed up as they arise. There is the opportunity for flexibility. The schools' attempt to give a broad education necessarily leads to children being trapped in a grid. Schools have to attempt to offer a broad education because they are trying to develop different aspects of very different people. This may seem like a benefit of schooling – how do you know if you have a young Nureyev on your hands if he never has the opportunity to dance? But my guess is that your young Nureyev would be dancing anyway and that a once-weekly music and movement class where he has to imagine he is a tree waving in the wind is going to make very little difference.

I can remember spending Monday mornings standing on a frozen hockey pitch waiting for my ordeal to be over and hoping that the ball would never come in my direction. I am indebted to those sports classes. I do not doubt they played their part in making me regard competitive sport with a loathing that I sincerely hope will be life long! When I think of the subjects I disliked at school – music is the only other one that comes to mind – I realize that I disliked the subjects that I was bad at and that school did very little to widen my interests, only to help me realize what I did not like. (Fortunately, my antipathy towards music vanished as soon as I left school.)

But still, it seems odd to me that I had the same amount of physical education at school as a future sportswoman would have had. And what use would those lessons in music have been to someone with real musical ability? Looking back at the lives of great musicians I see that many of them received an education that was strongly directed towards music, often from their earliest years. Although it seems a good idea to offer a broad education, as modern schools aim to, it does mean that children get stuck in a system that was designed to fit some idea of an average, ill-suited to the real needs of the individual.

A child can learn at her own pace at home. Gone are the problems of faster children having to be bored while the rest of the class catches up or of confused children unable to keep up or understand what is going on. I have read various different estimates of how much of their time in school children of various abilities are wasting. One educational psychologist, L.S. Hollingworth, suggested that children with an I.Q. of 140 waste half their time in school while those with an I.Q. of 170 waste virtually all their time. Judging from some of the telephone calls I have had from parents of children of average or lower than average ability, I begin to wonder what proportion of children school actually is aimed at.

On a practical level, being able to tailor the education to suit the child has obvious benefits. At home you don't have to go through every stage of everything to ensure that thirty children can follow it. You might be able to see straight away that the child you are working with has made a mental leap and can do without several intermediate steps. Or you may have to linger at a particular stage for as long as necessary.

But there is another level, equally important I feel. In my first chapter I mentioned the idea that small children need to be left to their dream-time and should not always have their attention directed by education-orientated adults. Childhood has lessons of its own which need no teacher. The need for time and space for thought and exploration is not just confined to infants. Young people, too, benefit from not having most of their thinking time appropriated by others. T.S. Eliot suggested that the ordinary processes of education 'consist largely in the acquisition of impersonal ideas which obscure what we really are and feel, what we really want'. Schools channel children's attention towards those things, those ways of thinking, that fit in with the methods of teaching that go on there. I suggest that home education offers more than the opportunity to give instruction to suit the needs of the individual: it gives the individual the time and freedom to fashion for herself the education she needs.

Religious Considerations

Parents with strong religious beliefs, whether based on a mainstream religion or a more personal view, may have firm ideas about the religious education they want their children to receive. The law recognizes the parents' right to decide this and therefore allows them to remove their children from religious classes that conflict with their beliefs. However, the L.E.A.s are bound by law to give religious instruction in schools so parents are forced either to accept the instruction given or to take positive action to avoid it.

Keeping a child out of these classes is not a satisfactory solution for many parents. One confirmed atheist I know, although she did not like the idea of her child being taught religion, did not want to put her in a position where she was made to feel an outsider because of it. She felt this would soon happen if her daughter, alone, was excluded from assemblies, Christmas concerts, plays and so on. Besides, she felt, the whole primary curriculum was infused with religious ideas.

The solution for members of the major religions might seem to be to track down a school run by their particular denomination but even this isn't as straightforward as you might think. Even if parents have such a school near at hand, they still may not accept its methods of teaching in their entirety. There are many differences of understanding within all religions, resulting in different attitudes to various aspects of life. For such people, Rousseau's advice is particularly appropriate:

> 'But who must train my child?' 'I have just told you, you must do it yourself.' (*Emile*)

My personal view (Victor's, too) is that children should be

given the freedom and encouragement to find their own beliefs. As a result of this, in our family there is – I hope – no inculcation but, rather, information and discussion.

Loss of access to the 'Great Outdoors'

Children are ill-suited to sitting still for long periods as most primary schools now recognize. It is wrong to have children confined to a classroom for the greater part of the day during most of their childhood. It is vital that children have frequent access to the outdoors if they are to have a real awareness of the world. Schoolchildren do get the occasional outing in schooltime but I wonder to what extent they carry with them the restricted view of the world their classroom walls give.

We went to see the West Kennet burial site near Avebury and Silbury Hill. Two school parties arrived while we were there. Both sets arrived by coach and had packed lunches and cameras. They had clipboards with sheets of questions to answer, which initially struck me as being rather a good idea. I briefly pictured Hosanna with a clipboard, busy observing and noting. Each party provided an interesting contrast both with the other party and with our own children. They were all about the same age, maybe a couple of years older than Hosanna.

The first set was from a private school, I would imagine; they were all boys. They sat in the hot sun, all of them with their blazers on, and listened to a lecture from Sir. They wrote things down as he talked, as if he was giving them the answers to their set questions. Class dismissed, a few took out their cameras, took some shots of their friends and then they all sat and ate their sandwiches before going back to their coach.

The second set were from a co-educational school. They came along like the previous school, in a crocodile, but were chattering more noisily and some were straggling behind. They also sat in the sun, but took off their sweaters and tended to chat up Sir rather than be lectured by him. There the difference ended. They also filled in the answers he gave them, took out their cameras, took a few shots of their friends and ate their sandwiches before going back to their coach.

A few of them ventured inside the burial site but most did not. When we went in, a couple of children were cracking jokes in the dark but they were talking of things other than burial mounds. No one seemed to look around them much. No one seemed particularly struck by the view – perhaps it was not mentioned on their clipboard sheets. Not one of them walked along the length of the mound. It did strike me that they were probably having a nice day out away from school, but where they were seemed immaterial.

Our own children spent a long time sitting in the gloom of the grave, talking about how things may have been long ago, what may have taken place there, what it might have felt like to have lived in those times. They talked to each other, and to us, about the stones at the entrance and the work that went into the construction of the site. They looked at Silbury Hill, the way the road curved round it, the surrounding countryside, the way towards Avebury. They spent a lot of time exploring the outside of the mound looking for 'evidence of man' – their own idea – turning over small stones, optimistically looking for axes or arrowheads. This evolved into a game. Meanwhile, the two separate school parties had come and gone, one after the other.

Victor and I sat on the grass and ate our sandwiches. There was no deliberate education going on. There were no answers to fill in. We had no lecture to give. Maybe schoolchildren would have felt that the sort of thing Hosanna and Fiorin were doing was too naïve and silly but our children thoroughly enjoyed themselves and came away with a real feeling about the place that no lesson on prehistory could have captured. We were quite content to sit in the sun and let our children play.

Being free from the restrictions of school hours gives us more opportunity to spend time out of doors. As we still do not live in the country we have to make do with walks and days out. For longer stays away, we are fortunate in having access to a shepherd's hut – a wheeled structure a shepherd would once have used to be near his flock – that has come to rest on a small, secluded plot in Hampshire. There we spend very primitive holidays, cooking, eating and often sleeping out of doors. The children leave their toys at home and spend their days making games with sticks and whatever else they can find. They do a lot of walking. They help to fetch water, light fires, prepare meals. They chat to the rare passers-by, who are pleased to stand and talk. There are horses, goats and donkeys to visit, wild rabbits to watch, minnows to catch in the river Test nearby. On wet days they can get out the books that Victor and his cousins read when they were children – still there on the shelf above the bed. Every spring Hosanna and Fiorin look forward to the break in the weather that signals that it is time for the first visit of the year to the Shepherd's Hut – regardless of school terms and timetables. It hardly needs to be said that not only do they enjoy it and never want to return to Bath, but it is a valuable and thoroughly 'educational' experience.

The Poetic Spirit

Linked in some ways to what I have said above about being in touch with the outdoors is the quality that we call the poetic spirit. I feel that schools unwittingly kill off a child's feeling for the poetic both in literature and in life.

First, let us consider poetry in itself. We have always been dubious about the teaching of poetry in schools. At the primary level, while I am sure there are some schools which do it well, my memories are of the most banal verse – only the worst was apparently considered suitable for children. By secondary school, many pupils had already got the message that poetry was boring and too difficult to make head or tail of. I was surprised to hear that, even on a degree course in English, there was a feeling among most of Victor's fellow students that poetry was of very little interest compared with prose. There were even poetry tutors who prefaced the courses they gave with an apology. The damage already done by schools was as bad as that.

We decided that the way to avoid this was to read the finest poetry to even the very smallest child. Getting a toddler to sit still and listen might seem to present a problem but that is not the way we go about it. We find that if we read to each other – or aloud to ourselves for our own interest – the small child will, instead of running off, draw close to hear more, ask questions, ask to hear that bit again. The idea is not to bombard her with it but to allow her to share in this enjoyment if she wishes to. If you really enjoy it, the chances are that she will soon want to be part of whatever is going on. It does not matter how difficult the poetry is – my children at age three would creep closer to hear *Paradise Lost* – they take it in without needing to decipher every word. I found this was so even reading them Chaucerian English. They do not baulk at it or say they do not understand. They draw from it what they can. I wonder if they will at a later age suddenly decide poetry is all too much of a struggle but I somehow imagine they will not. Hosanna now lies in bed at night reading poetry – not just children's verse – to Fiorin, who listens with rapt attention.

One evening, when Fiorin was not yet four, she asked me to tell her a poem. I went through my small repertoire of those I know by heart and recited to her, after a few others, one she had not heard before, John Webster's poem, *A Dirge*:

> Call for the robin-redbreast and the wren,
> Since o'er shady groves they hover,
> And with leaves and flowers do cover
> The friendless bodies of unburied men.
> Call unto his funeral dole
> The ant, the field-mouse and the mole,
> To rear him hillocks that shall keep him warm,
> And (when gay tombs are robb'd) sustain no harm;
> But keep the wolf far thence, that's foe to men,
> For with his nails he'll dig them up again.

At the last two lines her eyes grew wide with a look of fascinated disbelief. 'Again', she whispered each time I came to the end. Over the next few days I had to repeat the poem many times. The only questions she asked about it were 'What's "hillocks"?' and 'What's "foe"?' Apart from answering these two questions, there was no further explanation or discussion. After a while the interest seemed to die down but then, apparently out of the blue, she came up to me a few weeks later and told me she had made up a poem about the funeral of a wolf. As she started to tell me her poem, I realized it was closely based on *A Dirge*, calling upon the birds and small animals to cover the body of the dead wolf, just as Webster's poem had said they covered unburied men. Not having a pencil to hand, I was not able to get all her poem written down but I did write down the last two lines:

> But keep the man far thence, that's foe to all,
> For with his spade he'll dig them up again.

Her whole poem was said smoothly and without the slightest hesitation. I know it would not be at all remarkable for a child of nearly four to quote back parrot-fashion some lines from a poem. It was not that aspect of it that impressed me. I did think it was remarkable, though, for such a young child to be able to take an idea – an idea that had not been commented on at all – and to invert it, skilfully weaving it into a parallel poem. Instead of Nature being sympathetic to man with only the wolf as the enemy, in her poem Nature was sympathetic to the wolf and man was the 'foe to all'. Not only had she thought it through logically but she knew exactly which words to keep – she obviously instinctively understood expressions like 'far thence' which she is not acquainted with – and which words needed to be substituted to fit in with her new meaning. Using a spade rather than his nails was a masterstroke, I thought – what better way of showing how far removed from Nature man really is: he doesn't even get his hands dirty.

This feeling for poetry extends to other things – the day at West Kennet is an example. They seem to be aware that just below the surface of the mundane is a rich seam, full of symbolism and meaning. They do not need to know what it all means – they recognize that this is not always possible. I notice their interest in things which some of our school-going friends dismiss with a shrug. Hosanna and Fiorin do not tire of hearing about the links between the mythical and the everyday. Talking to other parents with children out of school, I find that they notice a similar awareness in their own children, perhaps a deeper interest and feeling for history or nature or religion. The direction it takes probably depends on the family's inclinations.

What we call poetic awareness, in life rather than specifically in literature, was our major reason for not sending our children to school. We felt this sense of wonder at the world would be lost very quickly with constant exposure to the routine of the classroom. We did not want our children to be engulfed by a mediocre mass culture. We felt it was important that they should first have the freedom to develop their powers of discrimination and a sense of value in their own individual view of the world. Not all families would attach a great importance to this. But it has formed the basis of our learning at home together and is the one thing that we would be most loath to lose.

7

Obstacles and Objections

There are arguments against home education. I hope some of these will have been countered in the course of this book. In this section I aim to look at some of the questions which are raised about possible drawbacks.

Loss of parents' time

One of the main objections voiced by people I meet is that parents have to give up their time to educate their children. It is a matter of priorities. You have to consider what it is you want out of life. If extending the time you spend at home with your children is not at all part of your scheme of things then you might as well start looking at some of the positive aspects of school. Home education is something you take on because it seems right – because you want to. It does not mean that you have to sacrifice your life to have your children learning at home. The degree of your commitment depends on how many children you have, how young they are, how good a network of support there is, how each member of the family interacts with the others. There is a world of difference between having one teenager at home who knows exactly what goals in life she is working towards and having five young children, all clamouring for attention.

Having children at home all day can fit in more easily with some family circumstances than with others. Most families I know who have more than one child learning at home have a home-based parent. The amount of involvement from the other partner, if there is one, varies. There are families where the education is fully shared by both parents, who may also share the bread-winning role, families where a parent, usually the father, works full-time but does what he can to assist, as well as many families where one adult does it single-handed.

Where there are several younger children in a family, the parent may feel she needs to be at home anyway. Home education can sometimes seem like hard work in the early years but then so can life with babies or toddlers. Taking older children to school may mean getting younger children ready twice a day to take on the early morning and afternoon walk to school, or being left with a fractious non-sleeping baby or a recalcitrant toddler. When you meet your school child in the afternoon, she may then be tired, irritable and in need of your undivided attention. If you have the whole day to sort things out in, they may fall into a more comfortable pattern. Home education can make days together more positive and less just part of the daily round, the common task. Fortunately children do not spend all their lives looking to the parent to be their complement – things get easier as they get more independent.

In the families I know who have children learning at home, I do not get the picture of adults who have sacrificed their lives for their children. They often lead surprisingly full lives and are interested, lively people involved with many things apart from their children's upbringing. Some of the dullest people I ever meet are among those who cannot wait to get their children off to school. I certainly find I have far more freedom and scope at home with my children – and access to many more interesting people – than I ever had working in a limited environment like an office.

Burden of responsibility

It *is* a big responsibility. At times all the things my children need to learn about seem like a challenge but at other times I wonder how I will possibly manage to take on, for example, the equivalent of a secondary level curriculum, while juggling with a primary school age child as well as any future offspring. That feeling of being overwhelmed does pass, though, and I come back to the realization that we have to take it all a bit at a time.

I think it is a mistake to feel that you have to cover the equivalent of a school curriculum. Many lessons they have at school are made essential only by school itself. At secondary school, everything is split down into separate subjects which makes it seem as if there is more to do. Each teacher must have her area carved out and her value must be recognized, therefore she must have lessons in which to teach her individual subject. Do you need daily lessons in English or is your child getting plenty of English practice while she is finding out about Ethiopia – with history, geography and sociology thrown in too? Does she need weekly lessons on the Ancient Egyptians for half a term or did she learn just as much in those two days talking about the Egyptians after her visit to the British Museum? Or perhaps she found the visit a total bore and never mentioned it again – what good would weekly lessons on the Egyptians do then? There are subjects that need intensive individual study but they don't need the sort of slow weekly grinding away that they are given at school.

Still, it *is* a big responsibility. Sometimes you may wonder why you did not do it the easy way and hand over that responsibility to someone who gets paid for the job. However, as you had good reasons why you did not, these reasons are what will keep you going.

Can I cope?

It helps to realize that learning is going on anyway even when there is no teaching. I have been through periods when I have felt we have done very little meaningful education but I only have to look back at a piece of writing done a few months before to realize that progress is being made all the time even without our, the parents', conscious efforts. With very young children this progress can seem quite magical at times. With older children, because it is less dramatic, it tends to get noticed less.

Not everyone I know with children at home necessarily sees it as a commitment to be shouldered for ever. For some it is part of a short-term plan: one day school may seem appropriate. Perhaps a good way of looking at it is to take it a year at a time. If you think that your child will go to school later, you do not have to worry about her falling behind her peers and never catching up again. Raymond S. Moore and Dorothy N. Moore, authors of the American book *Better Late*

Than Early, argue that young children learn more through play than they will from schooling or formal lessons and they are helped rather than held back if they start school late. One example they give is of a boy who did not start school until 13, having had no teaching, but then overtook his classmates within three years. Of the 400 late-starters in their study, only four reported any serious problems but each of the four had been put in classes with younger children and forced to work their way up. The rest, who were put straight in with their own age group, soon caught up and, the authors say, showed a surprising unanimity of success and leadership in their later careers.

They also comment on a study carried out in the 1950s and 1960s in Michigan where children were accepted into school from the age of four in an attempt to find the benefits of early schooling. It was found that over a fourteen-year period nearly one third of the early entrants were poorly adjusted and three-quarters of them were considered to be entirely lacking in any qualities of leadership. Although the project was very popular with parents, keen to get places for their children, it was abandoned not just because it proved a failure but because the psychologists running the scheme came to see it as positively harmful to the children.

Educating your children yourself is, to a major extent, a matter of confidence. You do have things to offer your child. These may not be the conventionally accepted academic skills. If you have confidence in your abilities, whatever they are, that is one of the most valuable things your child can learn from you. Some of the cleverest or most talented people may be the most self-doubting. It is better that your child learns about her own worth under your care than that she picks up the idea at school that her abilities are of little value because they do not fit into the accepted mould.

Lack of resources

Parents may wonder if they can compete with the level of provision of teaching aids and materials in schools. The first point to consider is whether schools are as well equipped as we may imagine. We hear about shortages of books and equipment: in some places pupils have to share text-books and cannot take them home to work with. There is a widening gap between facilities in schools in wealthier areas and those in poorer areas.

My local primary school has what is regarded as a 'good' catchment area and I know that the parents take an active role in fund-raising and voluntary assistance in the classroom. I was mildly surprised when I went to look at the reception class a few years ago. I was not overwhelmed by what I saw. I saw the same sort of thing I had in my own home – home-made flashcards, home-made picture-word matching sets, home-made wallcharts, boxes of oddments for sorting and counting, plus books, paints, crayons, things for cutting, sticking, sewing, and so on. In other words, the usual sort of paraphernalia that you might well have accumulated anyway if you have young children and are vaguely interested in their education. It is not difficult to get together a wide range of materials for younger children. You do not have to be wealthy to do so. Like primary school teachers, you can make things yourself as the need arises.

The only glaring discrepancy I saw between my home-made materials and the school's was in my favour. For example, my picture-word matching sets were made to encourage close observation and careful discrimination. The teacher's home-made cards featured large pictures of fluffy animals. The five year olds were expected to match a pair of lilac chipmunks and distinguish them from green bunnies or goggle-eyed pink sparrows – and they were all a foot high. This is no exaggeration. These were the 'specialist' materials that awaited my child if she went to school. This quite cured me of the belief that schools are full of marvellous and suitable equipment.

Perhaps the situation is better at secondary level. Go and look at your local comprehensive school, preferably through the windows one evening during term time rather than on an open day when they are trying hard to impress parents. If it is anything like my local comprehensive, formerly grammar, school you may see the broken desks, the vandalized lockers, the pictureless walls, the bare and empty classrooms. Or perhaps it is like the well-endowed voluntary-aided school that I went to, which had a lot of equipment which I never saw in use.

We are assured that all schools have their own computers and that all schoolchildren have plenty of hands-on experience. My youngest sister left school in London last year. Her school had several computers, none of which she was ever allowed to use. And it wasn't that she wasn't interested: a home computer was one of the first things she wanted to buy when she left school. However, she was always in the wrong year for computer studies – not the wrong stream, even that might be understandable, but the wrong *year*. Now how do you get to be in the right year – forge a birth certificate?

Perhaps the equipment is there in schools; but its existence is of no value to the pupils unless they use it themselves or, at the very least, see it in use. I think people in educational circles are too often taken in merely by the fact that the equipment exists. They don't seem to realize that perhaps quite small numbers of pupils actually benefit from it. A local authority Education Advisor who went to see a friend about her home educated children suggested to her that she could not possibly provide her children with the sort of equipment that they would be able to use in school. The Advisor pointed out that the county had just bought a special electronic microscope that cost some fabulous sum of money, several thousand pounds. How could she hope to provide that sort of thing for her children? We might wonder how many children would actually get to use this wondrous instrument – there was only one in the whole county after all.

Even if we accept the argument that schools are well-equipped – and that is debatable – this brings us to question what benefit children actually derive from such equipment. This is my second point: how essential are these materials? So far, I might seem to have been saying that equipment matters. I think it certainly does in a school environment. A well-equipped school seems a better place to be taught in than a poorly-equipped school. But in a situation where real learning is taking place, special materials do not have the same degree of importance. Teaching aids facilitate teaching but not necessarily learning.

I am aware that there is a great deal of difference between the sort of work that goes on in the earliest years of schooling – helping children to read, write and count – and the work in a wide range of specialized subjects that goes on at the 'O' and 'A' level end of the scale. Looking back at my own 'O' levels, I have tried honestly to remember what equipment was used in the course of each. Apart from very rare use of film (television) and tape-recordings, which could be available in the home, most subjects called for writing materials and a source of information, either text-books or the teacher. The only subjects that required frequent use of other resources were art and the sciences. For art, I could come up with a wider range of materials today for my two children, just using the things we already have in our house, than I ever used in my years doing art at school or art school. Any family could provide most of the art materials that are available in schools.

So that leaves the sciences. Biology seems a particularly good subject to study away from the classroom. Physics and chemistry present a greater problem. For younger children, you can do quite a bit of science in the home using kits and household materials. There are correspondence courses that use materials that can be easily obtained. But I do agree this is one area where, if your child wants to do more than just get through the G.C.S.E., she will need access to laboratory facilities at some stage. Perhaps the local technical college could provide this: my local college allows 15 year olds to attend evening classes. Part-time attendance might also be the answer for science 'A' levels.

Personally, I remember the bitter disappointment of doing experiments at school. There was nothing adventurous or creative about any of it. Any slightly complicated experiment was done by the teacher while the class looked on. I hear that this is even more common nowadays in many schools, because of the lack of equipment.

You may feel there will come a time when your knowledge and facilities are outstripped and that your child will need lessons from someone with the specialized training that you lack. We find it a perfectly acceptable idea that our children may want to take formal lessons at some time in the future. It was never our plan to suggest that only we can provide them with all the information they will ever need. But every family and home has a pool of resources waiting to be tapped which will serve the needs of most children for a good few years. Most important of all, we have access to the real world and to the real people in it. Schools are not the real world. They have to compensate for this by using instead their equipment – their teachers, text-books, films, their lessons in life skills, housecraft, child-care, their community projects, their P. E. Schools may have much to offer, but, in offering it, they also take much away. Many of the processes children go through in school are only necessary because they are in school. They need to be taught largely because they are denied the opportunity to learn for themselves.

How can I hope to match the teachers' training?

It could be argued that teachers are the best people to teach our children as they have been specially trained for this. But just as equipment is only of value if the child learns through its use – it has no worth otherwise – the qualifications of the teachers are of little value unless the child is actually learning. Looking back, we can all remember teachers teaching away unaware that nearly all they were saying fell on deaf ears. Or perhaps they were perfectly well aware. Perhaps that is the system.

Recent reseach by Barbara Tizard and Martin Hughes shows that young children learn a great deal through quite ordinary family conversations at home and that the sort of casual talk that goes on at the dinner table is just as valuable as conversation that has a more obvious educational content. Their book *Young Children Talking* compares the quality of conversation at home and in school. Children at home have more opportunity to ask questions and are more likely to be able to take a lead in the conversation. In schools, discussions are often directed by teachers to achieve the ends that the teachers, and not the children, have in mind.

I came across an example of this recently on a television

programme about teaching. A mathematical problem was being discussed with some pupils. Just in case we missed the fact that the teacher was controlling the conversation, the narrator pointed this out to us – 'Note how she draws the right questions out of the children.' This was considered skilful teaching. But sometimes it is the *wrong* questions that will give us a greater insight into what the child understands. When the child knows that the wrong questions are unwelcome, she will learn to be inhibited about asking anything.

David Lewis' research on exceptional children (reported in his book *How To Be a Gifted Parent*, Souvenir Press, 1979) found that teachers do not value question-asking in the same way that parents do. In his study, parents and teachers were asked to arrange in order of importance ten characteristics of cleverness. Of the parents in the survey, 95% thought question-asking was highly important whereas this was placed in the *last three* by 85% of teachers. Teachers plumped for things like neat work and good school reports but these were rated as *least* important by over 90% of the parents. Given those findings, who do you think is best qualified to answer children's questions – the parent who welcomes questions even if she does not know the answers or the teacher who would frankly prefer fewer questions and tidier work?

Like parents, teachers don't know all the answers. Yet I recall a friend at school commenting that the difference between the pupils and the teachers was that we would say, 'I think. . . .' or 'I read somewhere that. . . .' even about something we knew, whereas the teachers would say the equivalent of 'This is so'. Is it that teachers believe they have to make statements of fact in order to gain credibility? Perhaps we carry through to adulthood the memory of their supposed infallibility. Perhaps this is why so many parents lack confidence and feel they have to rely on teachers to come up with the answers to their children's questions. As parents we don't need to keep a class of thirty under the spell of believing that we know all the answers. We don't need to keep the illusion going that we are the fount of all knowledge – our children know better than to believe that.

If we don't know the answers we can show our children the

way they can be found. It is not always possible – nor desirable, I think – to rush off and look up the answer at the precise moment the question is asked. While it seems commendable to do so, it would make the child realize that this is no ordinary conversation going on but an educational event. Better to continue an interesting conversation in a normal and relaxed way even if there are questions in it you don't know the answer to. In a conversation with adults you would not dream of rushing off to check up facts in books. If you feel you have to do this with your children, they would soon see that conversations with them are not considered valuable for their own sake but as a vehicle for education.

My feeling is that – before reaching for the books – it is better to admit that you do not know, to ask her what she thinks and to discuss the various possibilities you both come up with. And you can do this while washing the dishes or bathing the baby. I am sure that this line of approach is good for the child's confidence – as well as her ability to think. Always slavishly searching for the one right answer straight off will make the child feel that the answers she comes up with are inadequate – that her ability to understand the world is inadequate.

Am I a good enough model for my children?

The concern that I may not be as good a model for my children as I would wish has bothered me more than the thought that I would not have the expertise or knowledge to give them a good education. In the past I have sometimes wondered if they would not benefit from having a number of different influences on their lives, of which I would be only one. Nowadays I realize they get this anyway – they are not brought up in a vacuum. They see there are other ways of dealing with life, other things that people can do apart from what we do.

The idea that school offers other role models – particularly to girls who need to see that women can be something other than housewives or mothers – is not wholly valid. What role models are available in schools? So, children discover that women can be *teachers*! This is one of woman's traditional roles – an underpaid person who looks after children. We parents may not be conquering Everest, metaphorically, but neither are teachers.

I think that many people assume that if your children learn at home you have to be extraordinarily dedicated, patient and untiring. One of the reasons I wrote this book was to try and dispel this myth that you have to be super-human and preferably live on several acres on a hill somewhere, rearing geniuses and generally making everyone else feel inadequate. I live in far from perfect circumstances in a small house with a tiny garden on an urban housing estate – and on a very low income. I am not especially gifted or extraordinarily dedicated. Nor am I particularly patient – though I try! – or untiring. My children's education at home is one aspect of my life that gives me a great deal of satisfaction. I am convinced of its rightness and it does seem to me to be a success.

We all have our bad days. I get tired and lose my patience sometimes. I am not the most organized of people and sometimes feel threatened by chaos. My children forgive me for my occasional irritability and understand that today may not be such a good day but each day is different. I am sometimes surprised at their understanding and sympathy. Sometimes, if I apologize for having been tired or irritable, Hosanna will say in a matter of fact way, 'You're fine. Forget about it.'

It is especially difficult when we imagine wonderfully patient teachers in enlightened schools. It can make you wonder if your children are missing out. But teachers have headaches and off days, too. If you cannot always be in tune with your children – whom you love even though you may be unable to respond to them fully at this moment – how can a teacher always be in tune with the thirty children for whom she has temporary responsibility? Don't we all have memories of our teachers' foibles and failings? People may object that schools have changed a lot since our day but I find it hard to believe that human nature has changed so very radically. The teaching methods may have been modified to suit current thinking but the teachers are probably much as they ever were.

When you next see a television programme like *Teaching Mathematical Thinking* and wonder at the calm teachers, patiently waiting for the children to discover the answers for themselves, don't be fooled into thinking all schools are like that all the time. What you are seeing is an ideal picture of teaching. It is interesting to see the other side of school – the secondary school with its peremptory notices outside the classroom blocks instructing the pupils to Wait Here (in the rain?) until a teacher comes to accompany them inside, the junior school with the teacher barking far from patient orders. Talk to parents of school children. As Baroness Warnock said in the 1985 Dimbleby Lecture: 'There is almost no parent of children at school who does not have some educational horror story to tell.' (The *Observer*, May 24th 1985).

As Education Otherwise co-ordinators for our county for a few years, we heard quite a number of horror stories ourselves. One that always stuck in my mind concerned a five-year-old boy at an infants' school not far from here. His father had left home a couple of months earlier. The little boy had suddenly started wetting himself and had done this a couple of times at school. Then, abruptly, he took to wetting himself regularly at night and being very distressed about going to school at all. The mother had already explained to his teacher that he was very upset about his father's departure and that she thought this was the reason for his sudden insecure, regressive behaviour. Seeing her son becoming more upset and anxious about school, she decided to go and speak to the teacher again. She hoped that together they could sort something out that would help the boy through this difficult time. She asked to speak to the teacher privately but the response was that anything she had to say could be aired before the whole class. The mother was made very uncomfortable by this but persevered. When she commented that the day-time problem – the wetting – seemed to have sorted itself out, the teacher replied that he had soon stopped because she had smacked him each time he had wet himself.

The mother could scarcely believe her ears. This was the reception class of an infants school. This was a teacher who knew that the boy was going through a very difficult period.

This was in a county where teachers were supposed not to use corporal punishment – officially. The mother was there, after all, to find out what could be done about her son's sudden distress at going to school and she was stunned to be told this; to stand and hear this, having it publicly proclaimed, as she experienced it, in front of the class. Can we ever fully imagine how the child had felt?

I am sure most teachers would have approached the problem very differently. And I realize that not every parent would have been as shocked about it as this mother had been, or as I was. But it does bring home to me the realization that, if you send your children to school, you have little alternative but to accept the standards of behaviour of the teacher. If you are strongly committed to certain principles, you cannot expect someone else to abide by them; you can only expect a high standard of behaviour from yourself. You may not always live up to your own standards. You may not be the ideal parent you would like for your child but you should not have to put up with someone else's foibles, injustices or cruelties while you stand helplessly by.

Preparation for grim reality

Many people believe that unless children learn to take orders and to work hard, they will grow up unprepared for the harsh realities of life. Parents may look upon school as a suitable – and necessary – preparation for the world. But, again, school is not real life. As E. M. Forster experienced it: 'School was the unhappiest time of my life and the worst trick it ever played on me was to pretend it was the world in miniature. For it hindered me from discovering how lovely and delightful and kind the world can be, and how much of it is intelligible. ¯ . . .' (in a 1930s *Spectator* article).

There is nothing to say that if your child does not go to school, she is never going to do anything arduous. The degree to which she works depends partly on your expectations and partly on her self-motivation. I have heard of children imposing quite strenuous disciplines on themselves, working towards some self-imposed goal.

Most families expect their children to work in some way. I certainly do but I don't think this has to be grim to prepare them for some grim world. My view is that, if life is that bad, then they should at least have a childhood that is not borne down with drudgery and worries! There is plenty of time for the harsh realities later. Rousseau's words in *Emile* are as significant today in the uncertainties of our nuclear age as they were in the eighteenth century:

> Why rob these innocents of the joys which pass so quickly, of that precious gift which they cannot abuse? Why fill with bitterness the fleeting days of early childhood, days which will no more return for them than for you? Fathers, can you tell when Death will call your children to him? Do not lay up sorrow for yourself by robbing them of the short span which nature has allotted to them. As soon as they are aware of the joy of life, let them rejoice in it.

Some people take the view that children must be trained for the dismal, boring jobs which many of them will end up in. If you think this, even in these days of high unemployment, then perhaps you should prepare them for it by boring them now ('Begin early thus to harden her for disappointments, to moderate her desires. . . .' Fenelon, *Instructions for the Education of Daughters*, 1687).

But on a personal level, as parents, do we really have to accept that our children must be prepared to ask for so little from life? Perhaps you hope they will not accept a grim future. Seeing that there are alternatives to school may help them look for more satisfying alternatives in later life.

And then there is obedience. You will have your own views on how much unquestioning obedience you ask from your child. You may feel there are times when she will need to obey others. This was something I wondered about when Hosanna first went off to Brownies or riding classes. I wondered how she would take to being given orders, which other children get used to at school. But children have much more understanding and adaptability than we sometimes give them credit for. They are very quick to grasp that there are times when you do what somebody tells you – and fast.

I have heard the objection, from a headmaster, that children will grow up to be wilful if they are allowed 'too much' freedom, as he thought they might be if they learn at home – though I would have thought a child's experience of feeling frustrated and powerless at school might be a recipe for wilfulness, or even open rebellion. Having and exercising one's own will is not the same thing as being wilful.

Children need competition

Some people believe children need competition and think it is no bad thing that schools encourage and thrive on it. I notice men, particularly, express concern over lack of opportunity for competitiveness in learning at home. Could it be that this competitive drive is part of what is wrong with the world, that competition is a symptom of an insecure and self-destructive society?

Competition is only of benefit to those who have a chance of winning. Never mind the games ethos – all that 'better to have played and lost than to have never played at all' stuff – if children see that they don't have a chance of success they will often withdraw from the struggle altogether. Competition may encourage the top few to try harder but it signals to the majority at the bottom that they might as well give up. A teacher of mine used to extol the virtues of what she called 'gentle emulation' but this only works between people whose talents are roughly balanced to start with.

I cannot get out of my mind the small boy who, never having been singled out for being 'best' at anything at school, happened one day to be the 'best wobbly jelly' in the music and movement class, thus receiving a few moments of praise from the teacher. He recounted the episode to his mother repeatedly over a period of many weeks, unable to relinquish the memory of his unaccustomed glory.

Does competition even benefit the 'winners'? Sometimes they can pay a heavy price in tension, neurosis and self-doubt. Their self-esteem may depend so critically on being at the top that they may suffer anxiety about their worth if staying there is a strain. Without a competitive system, children can take pride in their achievements for their own sake, not because they managed to outshine anyone else. What really is valuable is the spirit of co-operation which can flourish once individual children no longer feel the need to score off each other.

Children learn from each other

Children do learn from other children. They also learn from their own actions and observations, adults, books and the world about them generally. Children in schools do learn positive things from each other but they also learn how to be mean-spirited, competitive, how to form into gangs and exclude others, how to bully or be bullied, how to put up defensive shields against possible mockery – and more.

One expression that gets bandied about a lot these days is 'learning from their peer group'. People seem to accept that this has come to mean 'learning from the set of children born in the same school year'. Surely, a child's peer group is not just confined to the thirty or so children who, by virtue of date of birth, happen to have been put together at school. A child's peers are her companions and equals – and I am not advocating cutting children off from these. They need and value the company of other children. But they do not need the intervention of adults in their relationships, overseeing them, directing them as to what they should be learning from each other. In other words, children need each other to play with and talk to, to be children with. They do not need the particular relationship that schools allow them.

School offers children wider horizons

I have discussed already how school offers far less equality of opportunity than it might seem to and how children may learn to accept the labels that schools place upon them. Children who have never had their confidence in their abilities crushed, who see that there are many paths in life apart from the well-trodden track that the majority go down, who have a strongly developed sense of their own individuality to go it alone when they need to are better set up for the future than those who come out of school with a few 'A' levels if they are lucky, or with perhaps no exam passes at all if they are not. Since most people do go to school, schools are bound to have their apparent successes. They can claim the credit for virtually everyone who, in modern times, is deemed to have succeeded in life.

What about G.C.E.s and G.C.S.E.s?

Some families whose children do not go to school reject the idea of working for examinations. For them, the paper-chase for certificates is part of the very system that they wish to avoid. Other families will feel that taking and passing exams is essential.

If she wishes to, a young person can study for G.C.S.E.s and other public examinations completely by herself. She will need to find out the regulations, syllabuses and set books from the appropriate Examining Board. She will also need to arrange with a local centre so that she can be entered for the exams when the time comes. The majority of private candidates prepare for the University of London Examining Board (see Addresses), for which there are examination centres throughout Britain as well as abroad.

Contact the local Education Officer for information about where the centres are and which Board's examinations they hold. If there is a technical college or college of further education nearby, this is another good place to seek advice. Their library should have copies of the regulations and syllabuses of the Boards that they prepare candidates for as well as copies of past exam papers. These can also be bought from the Examining Board. Past papers give a good idea of what sort of questions are likely to be encountered in the exam. Examination entrants are charged an administrative fee but no tuition fees need to be paid, of course. The set books sometimes change from year to year so a syllabus for the appropriate examination date must be consulted.

An alternative is to use correspondence courses. These will accept school age students. They send lessons through the post and mark and comment on the material sent back to them. They guide and advise students, as well as providing a framework for study. However it can work out expensively if the plan is to cover a number of subjects. Some people, having gained experience of studying for exams with a correspondence college, then feel more confident to tackle future exams by themselves. (See Nick Everdell's experiences in Chapter 9. Although he did his 'O' Levels using correspondence courses, he thought that very often the recommended text-books were so good that they would have been enough by themselves.)

Another alternative is part-time study at a technical college. My local college stipulates that young people wishing to enrol must have completed four years' secondary schooling – they agree that the equivalent at home is acceptable. This means that if the student is at fifth form level she can enrol for evening classes or for 'Flexistudy'. There might be a limit on the number of hours attendance permitted in a week: most colleges will not want to be seen to be competing with schools and so will not allow full-time attendance for school-age students. Apart from examination courses there are also some 'leisure' subjects, like French Conversation, that could be a useful and relevant supplement for a young person following a G.C.S.E. course at home. These non-examination courses are run by local authorities.

'Flexistudy' seems a particularly good idea for the home-based learner: the student works at home with correspondence course materials and attends the college for occasional tutorials. It is more expensive than regular evening classes but actually cheaper than working direct with a correspondence college.

I asked at my local technical college if they would let my daughter work with me in the language laboratory. They said she could (and that we could borrow the same language course – books and tapes – from the record section of the public library and do the course at home.) It is worth making enquiries to see what local facilities you can use: sometimes you will find there are lower age limits, sometimes the rules will be more flexible. Your technical college may also have computer facilities with teach-yourself programmes to which they may allow younger people to have access.

Most towns will have private tutors, some an organized tutor service, but personal tuition is going to be expensive. A couple I know, whose own children are learning at home, coach pupils from both state and private schools. Sometimes their students have been told by their teachers that they do not have a chance of passing an exam and so are not put into the exam class. Children who were 'written off' in this way not only pass but even get good grades away from the classroom.

In the G.C.S.E. examinations now being introduced for 16-year-olds, to replace both the G.C.E. 'O' Level and the C.S.E., there will be continuous assessment for those in schools but not for those studying for the exams at home. Instead there will be an extra paper. I have just read in the Education Otherwise Newsletter that the rumour is that G.C.S.E.s sat by external candidates will be more highly regarded than those by internal candidates, because employers and universities will have more faith in examination results than in course work assessment from teachers! Well, it's an interesting thought.

Many people do very well academically, studying at home. Passing public examinations in this way is far from impossible. But, even if you do not pass the desired number of exams, whatever that is, straight off at one sitting, life is far from over.

Those who do not get a good spread of examination passes at 16 are not barred from higher education for all time. Although at 18 they would have difficulty finding a place if they could not meet the usual entrance requirements, in their twenties they will have more opportunities as 'mature' students. They may find universities and particularly polytechnics and colleges of higher education willing to accept them without the usual qualifications as long as they can show willingness to study and suitability for the course. They will probably need to show evidence of academic work or ability to write essays. University and college staff know that mature students are very frequently more highly-motivated than younger students straight from school – they didn't just drift in because it was the accepted thing to do after the sixth form. They often get better results and are less likely to drop out.

You do not need any qualifications at all, of course, to do an Open University degree, working at home. Some places of higher education will accept O.U. credits in place of G.C.E. passes.

There is also the Access Studies scheme at colleges of further education for people with no qualifications: successful completion of an initial course guarantees a place on certain diploma or degree courses.

Education at home must be expensive

Over the past few years I have talked to a number of other parents who educate their children at home. Although several of these have lower than average incomes and might have difficulties keeping up with the cost of living generally, not one of them has ever mentioned the expense of home education. In contrast, some of the wealthier parents I have met – whose children do go to school – have remarked that home education must be prohibitively expensive. A friend of mine also commented on this phenomenon. She had noticed the same thing independently, that the people who object that home education is too expensive to contemplate are very often those who pay a small fortune for their children to attend private schools.

I have always tended to disregard the actual cost of having my children learn at home – if money were the major consideration, would anyone actually contemplate having a family in the first place? Although we live on a low income, we have not noticed a great deal of difference in the expenditure involved in educating a five or six-year-old as compared to a three or four-year-old. Since we provided books, paper, paints and outings throughout the early years, it did not occur to us to start counting the cost when school age was reached.

Besides, the money spent on educating at home is offset to some extent by the costs of attending school. Apart from the obvious ones, there are also hidden costs. Children herded together are subjected to pressure to conform. It is the children who go to school who are more likely to clamour for certain possessions that are all the rage. Children learning at home have less need to seek status through possessions.

Children are expensive. During a visit from an Education Advisor, one home educating parent I know listed all the many classes and functions her children attended every week but the Advisor retorted that a good parent does all that anyway – as well as sending her child to school (supplementing an incomplete education?) That is worth bearing in mind when you count the cost of home education.

However – and now to the negative side – if your children are going to sit G.C.S.E.s and 'A' Levels, it will cost money. Even if you do it all yourselves, you will have to buy set books and pay for examination fees, which would be free if they were at school.

Families may lose out financially, in that they may lose certain benefits they might be entitled to if their children went to school. Low income families lose their right to free milk and free school meals which their school age children would get during term-time. (Parents of home-educated physically or mentally handicapped children can claim for milk tokens.) After the age of 16, they stand to lose more as L.E.A.s give grants to low income families to encourage children to stay on at school – not for the home-educated, alas.

Parents of young people who stay on at school after the age of 16 continue to receive their Child Benefit payments. In the past, home educating families were likely to lose their Child Benefit because their 16-year-olds were not attending school – even though they were still continuing to learn at home as before. Lynette Cameron, a mother who found herself in this situation, decided to fight the decision on the grounds that her Local Education Authority had recognized that her children were receiving a full-time education at home. Mrs Cameron managed to persuade the Social Services Secretary to change the law on this point. In April 1986, the Government announced in Parliament that they were introducing an amendment to the Child Benefit Act so that parents of home-educated children could continue to receive Benefit in the normal way until the 19th birthday.

However, it seems that they are only extending this to families whose children were educated at home before their 16th birthday with the approval of the L.E.A. This means that families who have not been approved by the L.E.A. – perhaps because they have just returned to this country after living abroad, or because their child decided to study at home shortly before or after her 16th birthday, or for whatever other reason – will be refused Child Benefit. Also, as it stands at the moment, those families where a child reached the age of 16 before the Bill became law (on 28th July 1986) will still not be entitled to it. And that includes Lynette Cameron and her family as well as a number of others.

8

Home Education and the Law

The rights and duties of parents

Many people are under the impression that school is compulsory – that most of us do not have any choice other than to send our children to school. This is not true. *Education* is compulsory for children between the ages of five and sixteen but school is not. British law places the responsibility for children's education with their parents. Most parents delegate this responsibility and send their children to schools to be educated but an alternative is allowed for in the law.

The 1944 Education Act, as amended by the 1981 Education Act, states in Section 36:

> It shall be the duty of the parent of every child of compulsory school age to cause him to receive efficient full-time education suitable to his age, ability and aptitude, and to any special educational needs he may have, either by regular attendance at school or otherwise.

The phrase 'or otherwise' clearly allows for education other than at school. It is under this section that parents exercise their right to educate their children at home. It was no mere accident that the words 'or otherwise' were included – there is no loophole there that parents use to get round the law. It is important to bear this in mind: it is a legal right, not something about which you have to avoid detection or be granted special permission for. 'Otherwise' is one of the options open to parents just as school is. Alternatives to school were considered and allowed for when the law was drawn up.

Section 76 makes it clear that it is the parents who have the right of choice over their children's education and that the education authorities must respect the parents' wishes:

> In the exercise and performance of all powers and duties conferred and imposed on them by this Act the Minister and local education authorities shall have regard to the

general principle that, so far as is compatible with the provision of efficient instruction and training and the avoidance of unreasonable public expenditure, pupils are to be educated in accordance with the wishes of their parents.

Generally this section is interpreted in relation to the parents' choice of school but, taking into account Section 36, this underlines the idea that the parents are responsible for the education of their children in a wider sense.

The principle of the rights and responsibilities of parents is further endorsed in European law. The Protocol to the European Convention for the Protection of Human Rights and Fundamental Freedoms, Article 2, March 1952 states that:

No person shall be denied the right to education. In the exercise of any function which it assumes in relation to education and to teaching, the state shall respect the right of parents to ensure such education and teaching is in conformity with their own religious and philosophical convictions.

This has been ratified by Britain and therefore should be enforceable. It has not yet been put to the test by any family with children educated at home but there is a case currently being prepared for a family in Gwent.

The United Nations Universal Declaration of Human Rights provides us with another statement regarding the rights of parents, although this is a declaration of intent not a law and, as such, has no legal force in Britain. Article 26 states:

1. Everyone has a right to education.
2. Education shall be directed to the full development of the human personality.
3. Parents shall have prior right to choose the kind of education that shall be given to their children.

These foregoing quotations clearly agree on the principle that parents can determine what sort of education their children should have.

So far only the rights of parents have been considered,

rather than the rights of the children themselves. Children are entitled to education but, under the law, they have no right to determine what form that education should take – unless they are the subject of a Care Order.

However most parents contemplating educating their children at home would probably do so with the co-operation and agreement of their children. I do not know of any parents who are keeping their children out of school against the children's wishes. I have sometimes been asked – usually by people opposed to education at home – how I can justify depriving my child of the choice of going to school. My children *do* have a choice – they choose to learn at home. It is the other children, those who go to school, who have no choice in the matter. I was asked this question by a representative of the L.E.A. and when I replied that they had a choice, that they could go to school if they wished to but they chose to stay at home, the Officer looked shocked and asked how I could possibly consider a child's choice as being valid in such an important matter! So much for choice! I would imagine that a disapproving L.E.A. might wish to bring the matter of the child's opinion into the discussion only if it concurred with their own view, otherwise it would be dismissed as an irrelevance, as happened in our case.

It is sometimes assumed that you can only teach your children yourself if you are a qualified teacher. There is nothing in the law to say that parents need to have teaching qualifications – or any other qualifications for that matter – in order to educate their children. The requirement is that you can give your child access to 'efficient full-time education suitable to his age, ability and aptitude.' However these terms are not defined in the law and so must be open to interpretation.

In a recent judgement, efficient education was defined as 'achieving what it sets out to achieve'. Bearing in mind, for example, the numbers of children who leave school barely able to cope with the basic skills in mathematics and English it would appear, by this definition, that many local authorities are themselves in breach of the law. In Britain about one in ten adults has a serious literacy problem. In America, one third of all adults cannot read well enough to cope with newspapers or even poison warnings on bottles (figures from *Woman's Hour*, B.B.C. Radio, May 1986). Research at Lancaster University suggests that at least seven million people in Britain, about 13% of the population, are illiterate (*The Guardian*, 3rd February 1987). These figures were reflected in a *World In Action* poll conducted by MORI (Granada Television, 2nd February 1987) whose results show that 52% of teenagers and 44% of adults could not understand the instructions on a fire notice; 44% of teenagers and adults could not understand a bus timetable. Approximately a third could not work out a simple percentage problem (what number is 50% of 180?) and a quarter could not fill in a basic job application form.

The former Education Secretary Sir Keith Joseph was reported in *The Guardian*, 2nd August 1985, as having said that 40% of school children reap little or no benefit from 11 years of compulsory education. That figure is now freely used on television and radio as an acceptable estimate of the proportion of children whom school has failed to educate efficiently. Clearly schools themselves are not efficient even at achieving what they set out to achieve, let alone at offering education for 'the full development of the human personality' as the United Nations Declaration puts it.

The hours required for L.E.A. schools are outlined in the State Schools Regulations. They specify at least three hours 'secular instruction' daily for five to eight year olds and at least four hours for those over eight on at least 200 days each year. However these rules are intended for state schools only and do not even apply to independent schools. Nor should these hours be considered as a requirement for children taught at home. More appropriate perhaps are the hours outlined in the *Manual of Guidance (Special Services 1)* produced by the Department of Education and Science. This states that in home education schemes provided by the L.E.A.s for children who are unable to attend school there should be a maximum of five sessions a week, each session lasting one and a half hours for under eights and two hours for children of eight or older. These are recommendations and are not enforceable by law. However they provide an interesting guide as to what the

D.E.S. regards as desirable and some parents may wish to bear these in mind. Many parents will feel, though, that learning at home cannot and should not be broken down into a set number of hours of daily 'instruction', that the whole idea of such a thing is incompatible with child-centred education or with the natural process of learning which it could be argued goes on all day. But then they could say that their children's education was truly full-time.

The very word education is not defined in the Act. It has, however, been defined in court recently as 'The development of mental powers and character and the acquisition of knowledge through the imparting of skills and learning by systematic instruction'.

No guidance is given in the law as to how to determine what is suitable for a child's age, ability and aptitude. It is not a legal requirement that the education provided at home should follow the same syllabus as might be provided at a school, nor that it should meet any standard laid down by a school or the local authority.

Since Section 36 of the 1944 Education Act allows for education otherwise than through attendance at school it seems odd that the phrase 'compulsory school age' is used in that same section. Perhaps 'compulsory education age' would have been clearer. For children not at school this stretches from their fifth to their sixteenth birthday although L.E.A.s are not obliged to provide schooling until the term following the child's fifth birthday.

Further legal considerations

The law imposes certain obligations on the education authority. Section 37 of the 1944 Education Act states:

> If it appears to a local education authority that the parent of any child of compulsory school age in their area is failing to perform the duty imposed upon him by the last foregoing section, it shall be the duty of the authority to serve upon the parent a notice requiring him, within such time as may be specified in the notice not being less than fourteen days from the service thereof, to satisfy the authority that the child is receiving efficient full-time

education suitable to his age, ability and aptitude either by regular attendance at school or otherwise.

This section obliges the L.E.A. to ensure that all children in their area are receiving a satisfactory education. It has been argued by some families that the L.E.A. has no right to intervene unless it has cause to believe that the education provided at home is unsatisfactory. The law certainly states that the parent must satisfy the authority that efficient full-time education is taking place '*if* it appears . . . that the parent . . . is *failing* to perform the duty imposed upon him' (my italics). The argument is that if parents are not appearing to fail then they are under no obligation to satisfy the L.E.A. However the law is not clear on this. It might be argued that this suggests that the L.E.A. has the right to ascertain whether parents are failing in their duties. Most parents accept that if they are not going to send their children to school they will at some time almost certainly be asked to show the L.E.A. that education is going on.

Now we come to the problems. I must put a warning in here so that the reader does not get unduly alarmed. Most parents whose children learn at home will not encounter them. Most L.E.A.s nowadays recognize the 'otherwise' option that is open to families. They do not automatically launch into the following procedure.

If a notice is served and parents fail to satisfy the L.E.A., they may then be served with a 'school attendance order'. If this is not complied with, they may eventually find themselves in court. (Sections 10 and 11 of the 1980 Education Act deal with the procedure the L.E.A. must follow in issuing an order.) If parents are summoned under Section 37 of the Act (see above), it is possible to argue the case for education at home as defence.

The argument for home education would not apply, however, for summonses under Section 39 which states that a child who is registered at a school must attend it:

> If any child of compulsory school age who is a registered pupil at a school fails to attend regularly thereat, the parent of the child shall be guilty of an offence against this section.

If a child is registered at a school then she must be deregistered before the parents can legally undertake her education themselves. This is an important difference which parents contemplating withdrawing their children from school should be aware of.

Northern Ireland and Scotland

Education otherwise than through attendance at school is allowed throughout the U.K. In Northern Ireland the Education (Northern Ireland) Act 1947 contains sections identical to those in the 1944 Education Act. In Scotland there are parallel sections in the Scottish Education Act (1980), Sections 30 and 28 of the Scottish Act corresponding to Sections 36 and 76.

Dealing with the Local Education Authority

In a book on education I was reading recently, published in 1973, I came across a paragraph on education at home. The author said that only one parent, as far as he knew, had ever decided to allow her children to learn at home without formal instruction, and that was Joy Baker. She had fought Norfolk County Council for eight years, during which time she was fined, sentenced to imprisonment (which she avoided on appeal) and threatened with the prospect of her children being made wards of court. The author concluded that 'the moral of this is that you can refuse to send your children to school provided that you are prepared to fight the authorities for at least eight years'. (*Home and School*, Tyrrel Burgess, Allen Lane.)

Even if that was so in 1973, it is certainly not true now. The attitudes of many L.E.A.s have changed radically since then – forced by the number of parents deciding that their children can learn at home. I do not know just how many families nowadays are doing much as Joy Baker did with her children – but with none of the problems from the L.E.A. that she had to endure. If the organization Education Otherwise has 1,800 member families, my very rough estimate is that there may be a thousand families with school age children learning at home.

I may have underestimated on this. There are something like 8,000 children not accounted for either in state or private schools, or in institutions. Although I am not saying they are all happily learning around the family hearth – I am sure a number of them are not – it gives us a very different picture from the one Tyrrel Burgess saw in 1973.

The L.E.A.s are certainly not pursuing this number of families through the courts. I know of only a few cases where there is anything like a legal battle going on. The vast majority of families whose children are home educated do not run into any legal problems.

We as a family decided that it is best to co-operate with the local authority where possible rather than to seek confrontation. Although principles do matter, I considered that our principles were mostly our concern and that there was no point in feeling outraged if a representative of the L.E.A. saw the matter in a different light.

If you embark on home education, it might be a good idea to find out what attitude your L.E.A. is likely to take. You can do this directly or indirectly. I know of people who have telephoned their local Education Office to ask what the procedure is. They have then gauged from the response how relaxed they can be themselves in their approach to the authority. This is fine except that the L.E.A. is a complicated structure – the person you get through to may not be someone who really knows the county's policy. The clerk who answers the 'phone may agree with you that you are fully entitled to educate your own children and you may be lulled into a false sense of security. The senior policy-maker may hold quite a different view.

You would probably get a better picture of the likely response by finding out how other people in your county have fared. To do this, contact your local Education Otherwise Co-ordinator. Her address will probably be available from the library in the register of local clubs and societies or from the Citizens Advice Bureau. Failing that, you can find the address or telephone number of your local Co-ordinator from the E.O. central address (see page 196). She will probably be a parent with experience of home education with her own children and she will be likely to know what response various members in the area have had from the L.E.A.

If you are considering withdrawing a child from school, read the section on deregistration below. This is important as the legal situation is different when a child is registered at a school.

First, however, I will outline the usual procedure for a child who has never been to school. You may decide not to inform the L.E.A. of your decision and to wait until they find you out. You are not actually legally obliged to inform them – the onus is on the authority to make sure all the children in its area are being educated, not on you to tell them. I know a few people in various counties who feel that the longer they are undetected, the less time they have to worry about satisfying the authorities. They see no reason in drawing their case to the attention of the L.E.A. who may be overbearing and interfering.

My own feeling is that a good relationship with the L.E.A. is important and it is worth fostering this from the start. There may be neighbours who will not approve of what you are doing and 'shop' you, or callers like Health Visitors who may see it as their duty to report cases where children are obviously not attending school. This could get you off to the wrong sort of start. The Education Welfare Officer who is then likely to take up your case usually deals with social problems like truancy. To me it seems best to approach the L.E.A. from the outset as a caring parent who wishes to keep responsibility for her children rather than risk being reported as an encourager of truants.

You can inform them of your intention by a brief letter to the Chief Education Officer of your county. The format suggested by Education Otherwise, quoted earlier, runs:

> We write to inform you that, after careful consideration, we have decided to take responsibility for the education of our son/daughter . . . aged . . ., in accordance with our duty under Section 36 of the 1944 Education Act, otherwise than through attendance at school.

You may get a reply speedily (we were telephoned a couple of days later) or you may have to wait for up to several months. Some L.E.A.s now send out a standard form. Our county devised one when they realized there were going to be more than just one or two families doing this. Although we did not receive one, we did see a copy of the form sent to those families who came after us. The form presupposed the use of tutors, timetables and a set curriculum and it required much careful thought as to how to fill it in without looking as if their demands were being accepted in principle. To counter this, our friends sent back a covering letter outlining their aims and intentions along with the form with 'not applicable' written in many of the boxes. It is important not to be cowed by the L.E.A. but to stand your ground.

Be wary of committing yourself to a timetable or a set curriculum. Apart from anything else, it could be seen as an invitation for them to check up that you are actually sticking to it! Unless you know you are going to, it doesn't seem a good idea to say you will. There is no legal obligation for a set timetable or teaching qualifications and you certainly do not need to supply references. Obviously you will decide how much you wish to comply or compromise. In some cases, parents see nothing wrong with informing the L.E.A. of their intentions regarding formal instruction. Other families will see it as totally inappropriate.

Deregistration

If your child has never been to school you have no problems about deregistration. Even if you have put your child's name down for a certain primary school, don't worry – she is not registered until she actually attends.

If your child has been attending a private school of which she is no longer a pupil and she is not yet registered at or attending a state school, you do not need to worry about deregistration. Similarly, if you have just returned from abroad, deregistration is not applicable.

But if you want to withdraw a child from school in order to educate her at home, you first have to get her name removed from the school register. This can be a perfectly straightforward procedure, but it partly depends on your child's headteacher. She can simply remove your child's name from the roll at your request or keep her registered while reporting you to the L.E.A.

The problem is that if your child is registered at a certain school, you are legally obliged to see that she does attend. Although education elsewhere – at home, for example – will be grounds for deregistration, the L.E.A. may argue that home education is not taking place if the child is actually registered at school. During term time this can present a parent with a paradoxical situation: how can you start home education if your child must attend school? How can you say that home education is taking place if they will not let you deregister? It is suggested that, to avoid this problem, the school holidays are the best time to begin: by the next term the child's education at home is already underway and deregistration should take place.

Automatic deregistration

If you happen to move home either out of the area covered by your L.E.A. or far enough away from your child's school to make attendance difficult, your child will automatically be deregistered. The headteacher may well contact you to find out to which new school she should be forwarding her records. However she still has to deregister the child.

At the end of primary or middle school education, your child will be required to change to another school. If you have not accepted the place offered by the L.E.A., the child will be deregistered when she finishes at the lower school.

Procedure for deregistration

If you need to deregister your child, your first step is to write to the headteacher asking for her name to be deleted from the school roll. Your previous relationship with the school will decide to what degree you explain your intentions. Some people vaguely indicate that their child is going to be educated privately but the school will often get in contact to ask where they should send the child's records.

The headteacher may remove your child's name but will very likely inform the L.E.A. who may send round an Education Welfare Officer to find out what is going on. Experiences with these officers vary. The two who have been to see us over the years have been very friendly, helpful and not at all disturbed by the principle of learning at home. One even assured us that this was the direction education was going to take in the future and that we should apply for peripatetic teachers and books from the schools!

However other people have found that E.W.O.s have not been helpful and that it is better to deal direct with the Education Advisors. An E.W.O. is not trained in educational matters. Some have qualifications in social work and, because of their training and working experience, may see you as yet another problem family.

If the headteacher deregisters your child all should proceed smoothly – you now have the right to be responsible for your child's education. Should she resist removing the child's name, you will find yourself in the potentially sticky situation where Section 39 could be brought to bear. This 'registered but not attending' category can cause problems. She may write to you asking for a fuller explanation while she reports you to the Authority. I know a number of people who have had this happen. In a couple of cases an E.W.O. came and read out to them an alarming-sounding letter issued by the Court Office, demanding that they should satisfy the L.E.A. that they were not failing in their parental duties. The people I knew stood their ground, gave their reasons and not one case came to court. One friend kept up a lengthy correspondence with the headteacher who was very persuasive but that child was also deregistered eventually.

As I mentioned above, it is recommended that you apply to deregister your child during a school holiday. If you have an urgent crisis on your hands, it might not be possible to wait for the end of term. If you can hold out until the holidays, there is said to be less likelihood of problems with deregistration. It has been argued that if you write between school terms to inform them that you have already undertaken your child's education, the headteacher is obliged to accept it as an accomplished fact and must then deregister.

What to expect

Although most L.E.A.s are reasonably co-operative, it is advisable to be prepared for the possibility of confrontation. It is important to make it clear – without being aggressive – that you know what you are talking about, that you are firm in your decision and are aware of your rights. It may be that the representative of the L.E.A. coming to see you has a very uncertain understanding of the law on this point. It may be new ground for her.

Keep a record of your dealings with the L.E.A., noting the name of any official who telephones or calls on you. You may never need to refer to this information but it is as well to have a record of your dealings with them in case any problems or misunderstandings should arise. You may wish to take notes when you are visited – it is easy to forget what a person said once she has left so take notes openly if you want to. We started doing this on our first visit from an E.W.O. He was not at all bothered by it – after all, he was taking notes, too. However it was not a practice that we felt the need to keep up.

You may first be visited by an E.W.O. or you may get straight to the next stage which is usually a visit from an Education Advisor. In different counties they may have different titles. This Advisor is the person who will probably ask you what work you are doing with your child. Her usual job may be visiting and advising schools.

She will probably ask to see examples of your child's work and may ask to hear her read. If you are going to show work, have it to hand. If your child is young and you know she will not read to a stranger, say so. Perhaps you would prefer the Advisor to listen while the child reads to you. Be guided by your own understanding of your child: do not allow yourself to be pushed into an unnatural situation which is going to upset her. She is your child. Where possible stay in control of what your child is asked to do.

Children and parents should not be put under strain by these visits. If you are not happy about discussing your child over her head, don't be drawn into doing it. On the other hand, don't send her out of the room at the Advisor's request if that's not the way you do things. Don't feel under pressure to prove anything: it is more important, I feel, that your child looks happy and unstrained than that she appears to be above average academically. At the primary level, parents may be likely to err on the side of too much of the three 'R's. The Advisor will probably want to see evidence of art and crafts, a wider curriculum than would be shown by pages of neat writing or correct sums. She is very likely to want to know how you compensate for the assumed lack of all that socialization children are supposed to get at school.

When we were visited by an E.W.O. when Hosanna was five and an Advisor when she was six, I very much bore in mind the expression, 'She is not a performing seal!' I was prepared to object if I thought she was being put through her paces – after all, no child coming to school is expected to know how to read, write or do sums. I decided that, at this stage, they would have to accept my word as to her abilities. However the problem did not arise – on neither of these visits was Hosanna asked any probing or testing questions nor was she asked to read aloud. By the next visit she was seven and a half. When asked by the Advisor if she had anything she would like to read, she quite naturally looked through the book she was reading at that time – I think it was *The Lion, the Witch and the Wardrobe* – for a passage to read aloud. I saw no reason to object as Hosanna was clearly quite relaxed about it.

I would be opposed to anything that started to look like formal testing by the L.E.A. – at any stage of my children's education. It is wrong to submit a child or young person to the sort of pressure that this could create; even children doing examinations at school are not being separated out for individual close scrutiny. Formal testing of home educated children is particularly inappropriate: apart from anything else, it is not fair to test a child within the framework of a system within which she has not been educated. Testing I.Q. or knowledge of what will inevitably be a few selected facts seems largely irrelevant and all assessments are open to misinterpretation. I cannot see that the law as it stands actually calls for the testing of children by the L.E.A. The 1944 Education Act states that it is the parents' duty 'to cause' their children 'to receive' suitable education and that the L.E.A. has a duty to check on any parent who appears to be failing in this. But there is nothing to say that the children are legally obliged to learn! We have said to our children before a visit from the Education Advisor, 'Don't worry: if anyone is being inspected, it's us, not you' and this does release them from any feeling of personal pressure. We see these visits as a check on the provision of education rather than on our children's abilities.

There may be certain rare circumstances in which the parents accept that formal testing is appropriate – though, under normal circumstances, I would certainly resist it unless it seemed to be of positive benefit to the child concerned. Some parents have come to an arrangement with the L.E.A. where any necessary assessment has been carried out by an independent body. If you get into this situation, Education Otherwise may be able to help by putting you in touch with educational psychologists – or other professionally qualified people – who are sympathetic to the idea of home education.

Once it is established with the L.E.A. that your children are going to learn at home and that you are not going to be dissuaded from this, it should settle into a pattern where you know what to expect from them and they know what to expect from you. It is likely that you will be visited annually – though there is a wide variation. I know of some people in other counties who get visited so infrequently that they wonder if their files have been lost. However, one family I read about in the Education Otherwise newsletter was visited at four-weekly intervals for the first six months after they withdrew their children from school.

A timetable and curriculum may be requested. In our county we are asked to send in a report on our children's progress periodically. Victor and I do not object to this though I know some people do. I find writing a report less of an imposition than over-frequent visits. And when we sit down to write the report, we clarify our objectives and see again where our weak links are.

Children with Special Educational Needs

Since the 1981 Education Act, handicapped children are no longer considered in different categories according to their disability but as children with Special Educational Needs. A growing number of these 'special' children are being educated at home. Their parents see the benefits of growing up and learning in a warm family environment, and this can be particularly important for children who might otherwise be segregated from the rest of the community. Sometimes they turn to home education because they are unhappy with the provision that the L.E.A. offers.

A handicapped child may be assessed by the L.E.A. and a Statement of Special Educational Needs may be made. The parents have specific rights with regard to this procedure. They can find out their rights and obligations by referring to the 1981 Act, which should be available in the local reference library. The Advisory Centre for Education (A.C.E. – see Addresses) have published the *Special Education Handbook*, which includes a copy of the Act.

Parents of children who have been assessed as having Special Educational Needs have certain limitations to their rights. In particular, if they have a child of compulsory school age who is registered at a special school, they may not withdraw her without the consent of the L.E.A. If consent is refused, they may refer the matter to the Secretary of State.

If you are the parent of a child who is about to be assessed for a Statement of Special Educational Needs, you may wish to try to negotiate to have home education included in the Statement. The 1981 Act states in Section 7 (2) that where an L.E.A. maintains a statement, 'it shall be the duty of the Authority to arrange that the special educational provision specified in the statement is made for him unless his parent has made suitable arrangements'. Education at home might be accepted as 'suitable arrangements'. If you are not yet sure whether to educate your child at home or not, remember that a decision to do so can be revoked – you can change your mind – whereas to withdraw her from a special school requires the consent of the L.E.A.

Families wishing to educate their 'special' children at home should get as much information and support as they can. There is an Education Otherwise Special Needs Support Group (see under Education Otherwise) through which families can contact others and get the advice and support they need. In the absence of test cases clarifying the 1981 Act, Local Education Authorities can vary in their interpretation of the law. This makes contact with other families in a similar situation particularly valuable.

9

Different Approaches

Most families whose children learn at home soon sort out their own approach to education and settle on the method and materials that suit them and their way of life best. Many would know exactly 'how to do it'. Others – perhaps particularly those who feel they have been thrown in at the deep end because they have had to withdraw their children from school – might welcome suggestions and ideas. But the best way of finding out 'how to do it' is to do it.

Talking to other families with children learning at home can be a valuable source of information. In finding out what worked or did not work for them, you may realize what it is that will work for your own family – although that might be something quite different. It is pointless trying to adhere to a school-type curriculum if it means that the whole family is constantly in a state of anxiety about keeping to it. On the other hand, it is pointless trying to adopt a 'let the children play' attitude if this is going to make you feel anxious – if really you are concerned that one day the playing has to stop. There are so many factors involved that there can be no one way that will be right for everyone.

Having embarked on home education, you may find yourself subject to other people's expectations. The L.E.A. may make demands for timetables, planned curricula and evidence of a parallel to schooling. You have to decide what degree of co-operation you are prepared to give. You may also get criticism from relatives, friends or neighbours who may openly disapprove of your decision or have firm views on the way you should be doing it all. I have been very fortunate in this. Our friends – even those whose children are at school – never try to convince us we are doing the wrong thing and more often reinforce what we are doing by pointing out the drawbacks of school. I know of other home-educating families, though, who feel that some of their friends are just waiting for the opportunity to say 'Well, why don't you send them to school, then?' This must be very dispiriting.

I have known of a few people with children out of school whose own parents, the grandparents, are very upset about the situation. As one person put it, 'Certainly our own encounter with the Education Board here has been a mere breeze, compared with the icy gales of disapproval from our families, all the harder to bear because they love the children too, and genuinely feel we are wrong.' Perhaps it is particularly difficult in cases where, as the grandparents see it, the children have been suddenly withdrawn from school. It may be easier where it was known from the beginning that school was not on the horizon. But you cannot live out other people's expectations. Even if others genuinely feel you are wrong, it is they who have to come to accept that you are doing what you genuinely feel is right.

Or you may meet quite a different problem: pressure to conform to some alternative orthodoxy. It does exist. A number of people who support the idea of children learning at home have very strong views on freedom and the unrestricted development of the individual. Many parents are very attracted to the idea that if you give a child freedom she will learn in her own time and in her own way. Sometimes this works out well. Children will learn a vast amount given the time and space. But it will not necessarily be what the parents had in mind or what they consider an adequate education – this may or may not bother you. Most children will learn to read, write and count, given freedom, but it is not every child who will educate herself totally under her own steam.

There is no point drawing parallels with somewhere like Summerhill where classes were optional. In any school, however free, there is still pressure to conform just by virtue of the fact that classes and teachers are there waiting in the background. Even if they are optional, the mere existence of lessons shows that there is work to be done. The child is aware of this even if she chooses not to do it. Obviously the happiest situation is one where children learn without coercion. We were talking about this to a couple with four children who learn at home. They lived in a wonderful country environment and their children were able to enjoy a remarkable amount of freedom and independence roaming the country-side. The parents remarked ruefully that they came to a point where they felt they not only had to introduce lessons but even to enforce them. They had originally hoped that their boys, the eldest of whom was in his teens, would one day naturally take up their books and decide it was time to become fully literate and numerate. But they came to realize that their children, given the choices available to them, were always going to choose fishing, biking and camping.

Ever since Locke and Rousseau, parents have been advised to train their children in husbandry, woodcraft and useful manual skills. The practical man has long been held up as a worthy example in alternative education circles as if this approach is somehow considered more respectable than the academic mainstream. If you are a carpenter or a needle-woman and you can see that your child has a 'natural' skill with wood or thread but a disinclination towards academic skills, then you may find it perfectly easy to be radical and to allow your child to pick up practical skills. But, nevertheless, you will probably show her the correct way to use a chisel or put in a zip. And you may rightly say you are doing it all naturally.

What if your skills happen to be mathematical or literary? What if you can recognize that your child has academic abilities? If throwing away the books but showing her how to use a lathe, to stitch, or cook, or pot, or rewire the house does not come naturally to you or her, then this would not be doing it the natural, radical way. Daily writing or reading or maths is as natural for one family as daily woodwork alongside Mum or Dad is for another. She needs to develop and practise her skills, whatever they are. Yet I have sometimes felt there is some sort of cult snobbery going on as if manual skills are the only mark of an acceptable alternative education.

In *News from Nowhere*, William Morris describes an ideal, a community where children pick up the skills they need:

> I can assure you our children learn whether they go through a 'system of teaching' or not. Why, you will not find one of these children about here, boy or girl, who cannot swim, and every one of them has been used to

tumbling about the little forest ponies . . . they all of
them know how to cook; the bigger lads can mow; many
can thatch or do odd jobs at carpentering or they know
how to keep shop . . . however, I understand you to be
thinking about book-learning; and as to that, it is a simple
affair. Most children, seeing books lying about, manage
to read by the time they are four years old.

Well, it would be truly wonderful if things always worked out
that way. However I think he is certainly optimistic about the
age at which children learn to read . . . and spontaneously.
However many books you leave lying around, the age when a
child learns to read of her own accord may be many years later
than that. Although there is much that is good and right about
Morris's approach it does serve to worry the parents of those
children for whom it does not all fall into place so happily.

Just as each family has its own character, each family will
evolve its own approach to learning at home, as the following
extracts, from Education Otherwise members, show. The
first account is from Primmy Chorley about life with her two
children, Joseph and Jessie, who were then aged nearly seven
and nearing four:

A Page From Our Diary   *Mon. Oct. 29th*

Patterns, gipsy caravans. Yesterday J and I made a small
gipsy caravan (wooden box on wheels) and Jessie and I
helped J to decorate it – today talked about gipsies then
and now and lifestyle and its changes, remembered all we
could of book of gipsy photos from library. All busy
making things to go in the caravan. Joey made furniture,
Jessie made a wooden settee/bed, mattress/eiderdown; I
wove a little mat. Crayoned carpets, peg-doll gipsies,
dressed up other dolls as gipsies. Then I helped Jessie to
convert a small farmhouse (made by me long ago) into a
gipsy caravan. Painting, crayoning and some woodwork
to convert it. Her caravan is for fairies. I embroidered a
carpet for her. Joseph writing about gipsy caravans. Play
with the caravans, travels, setting up camp, meals, horses
grazing etc. Making tiny tea sets out of paper. Entire day
spent on caravans. Magdalene came to play but J & J were

too engrossed in the caravan so I took her back. Walks in heavy rain and wind. Played unblocking streams in flooded water on the track. Listened to radio – music, *Science Now*, stories. Read Mr Rabbit story and the last chapter of *What the Neighbours did* (Phillipa Pearce); re-read *The Twits*.

Thurs. Nov. 1st

Drawing and writing, looked at books of birds, books of *Grey Rabbit*, elephant pictures by man and lady that lived with elephants for some years; sewing buttonholes, dressing up dolls, bicycle ride. Colours out of doors, and changes. Saw a heron in a ditch just close to us. Explored the depths of puddles. Played fairies under the trees and continued the fantasy as we walked home. Counting the curtain rings. Talked about 'half'. Joey helped me to grate fruit and chop nuts for muesli. Jessie sewed a fairy's bag. Joey made a series of bags within bags to sew on his new coat and embroidered 'Joey' on them all. More drawing. Long walks with dog and found more toadstools to look up – very bright ones. Radio – *Medicine Now* and current affairs. Jessie crying for a real baby of her own. Talked about babies and age and death and a broken pelvis, cremation and burials. Grandmother story (collage pictures). . . .

For me this captures the essence of the very special quality of children learning at home – what primary school could match it? The account continues:

We've never had any toys (except some old passed-on cranes and lorries). We've made everything we use to play with from what's around us. To begin with, it was piles of logs and bits of wood and stones . . . Joseph has always known what he wanted to do, set things out in a particular way, had an eye for anything useful out of someone else's rubbish. . . . He started to learn to read by making huge letters from the tree prunings in the orchard and can now write very neatly and likes to draw ornate letters. He is on the verge of reading. Usually his machines need some names or directions written on them and inevitably we cover some history, geography and maths etc without the children ever knowing they are learning.

Perhaps some parents may wonder if this method of education is acceptable to the L.E.A. It is sometimes assumed that the authorities will be looking for evidence of formal work, a parallel to schooling. I found Primmy's account of how her family fared with the L.E.A. very interesting on this point. Shortly after they had moved to Wales they had informed the Education Authority of their existence in the area. They suspected they might be reported to the L.E.A. so they decided that they preferred to declare themselves and invite a visit – even though they were still in the process of working on their new home – rather than find themselves embroiled in any sort of misunderstanding in an area they had just moved into. They had already been visited once in the county they had moved from, without encountering any problems:

> I was equally nervous of this visit as the house was squalid, we'd only got the kitchen fixed, and one room useable but crowded, and to get into that room meant seeing all the rest of the mess. I covered the whole room in white sheets, bed and all and covered all the walls and surfaces and bed with Joey's wooden objects and drawings and made piles of all the writing. Then put all our usual daily muddle in the room as well, so the room became home for the day. Also decorated the wall around the front door with drawings and writing. The Education Officer's first words on meeting Joey were – 'You don't need to go to school do you!' He was very impressed with the display and stayed for 2–3 hours.

For the second visit a year later another exhibition of work was mounted:

> The Education Officer was amazed at the beautiful room, and the amount that Joey had produced – he said this was 'real' learning.

He made helpful suggestions, which fitted in with the family's approach to education. He was so impressed, he asked whether he could come back and take some photographs to show teachers.

Parents of even quite young children are concerned about the teaching of such subjects as mathematics. One Education Otherwise member was asked in a radio interview how her children would ever learn to add up if not in a classroom! Here is an account of how one mother, Betty Ball, tackled mathematics with her five-year-old son, Tom, through play. I should say here that she was herself formerly a maths teacher, but the approach she uses is within the scope of any family – my own living room has been converted to a shop or a cafe many times over the past six years or so.

> Tom loves playing shops and has a drawer of empty boxes within boxes, which he frequently covers the house in. Initially they were super for sorting work and we would sort the lounge into a chemist shop, a toy shop. . . .
> More recently the boxes have labels on and prices and he will make out bills for me and add them up. To start with I chose carefully so that there were no tens to carry but have more recently chosen anything. We played shops the other day and there was a sale on, everything was half price and he played for ages re-labelling them. He has also drawn notices for the door of opening hours, etc. For calculations, I keep a tin of money mainly 1p and 10p, and some toy £1 notes. In this way we have seen addition and subtraction work before we even wrote the calculations down. We put the money with the goods, add (or put) it all together and change 10 x 1p for a 10p piece. It makes sense that way.
> To do subtractions, if we want to do 341 – 125 we pile up the 3 x £1, 4 x 10p and 1 x 1p and try to take 125 away. If there aren't 5 x 1p to take away we change 1 x 10p into 10 x 1p at the bank of money in the tin.
> Another love is playing hospitals and I recommend being examined lying down on the settee when the housework

is wearing you out. The other day he wanted to play this so I suggested that real patients had temperature graphs at the end of their beds. Soon all the toy animals had theirs and we had begun to learn graphs and normal body temperature.

She aimed to follow her son's interests rather than to direct his education according to a curriculum. Soon after her initial contact with the L.E.A., a curriculum was requested but she stood her ground and explained that this was incompatible with her aim to follow an individual-based system. The response to this was a letter from the Primary Advisor expressing concern at:

the absence of any reference to imposed discipline. . . . Society as we know it, whether acceptable or not, does demand whether we like it or not both self-discipline and submission to externally imposed discipline. The development of 'stickability' despite one's inclinations is a necessary discipline of learning.

She was asked to make an appointment to see the Primary Advisor. Betty continues:

I attended with trepidation. I was not using any maths text book or scheme and much of my evidence of Tom's development I felt was in terms of conversations we had had together – with no evidence . . . she was pleased that I was not using a text book. She said that most parents teaching their own children ploughed through a text book because they thought it was what they would be doing at school but that understanding in real life situations was much better at this stage.
We also discussed at length how having relaxed into the situation of home education, I felt it less necessary to manufacture situations for learning but to use my son's interest. It really does just happen if you are receptive to their ideas. Also use of suitable games gives practice in arithmetic and logical manipulation without drudgery. All this she accepted and tended to agree with although she still wished work discipline to be there.

. . . About a week after this meeting, the Primary Advisor was talking on a training course for Playgroup Supervisors about Early Education. She told them about a group of parents called Education Otherwise who were interested in their children's education from birth onwards and the excellent work they were doing. This was reported back to me by a friend on the course and was very reassuring. . . .

Both this last paragraph and the response that the Chorley family had from the visiting Education Officer suggest that individuals in some L.E.A.s are in fact highly impressed with the results of education at home, although they might not necessarily appear to agree with the idea at first.

Families whose children have been withdrawn from school, for whatever reason, initially have a very different situation. They often find they have to go through a period of transition. Adults and children need to adjust to a new way of life together, and this can take time. Parents contemplating removing their children from school sometimes feel daunted by the task that lies ahead – all too often they feel they have to offer a parallel to schooling. Sometimes they start off exactly where the school left off, with timetables, textbooks and lessons. Perhaps because they think that this is what the L.E.A. will demand of them, perhaps because it seems the obvious way of going about things in an organized way. The new system may break down for a variety of reasons – possibly surprisingly quickly. Children may resist teaching or plainly fail to thrive as the parents had expected. The adult may find she cannot cope with this new full-time job as teacher or she may simply come to realize that, for her family, this is not the right way.

The following account by Jude Ashley-Walker describes this beautifully. She has four children, aged 16, 14, eight and four. She embarked on home education, originally prompted by a vicious attack on her eldest son – by a gang of eleven boys during a religious instruction class at school (the mind boggles) resulting in his needing treatment at the hospital. She was advised by the school that he should see an educational psychologist as he had been bullied regularly. The mother wondered if the gang of bullies were not the ones in need of a psychologist but she was assured their behaviour was 'normal': normal for school perhaps. The implications of this are very disturbing.

She received dire warnings – from the psychologist, the teachers, the headmaster, the Education Officers – of the consequences if she removed her children from school. She was told that the family would become isolated and neurotic, that her action was illegal, that she could not educate them herself as she was not a qualified teacher, that she could be sent to prison and that her children could be put into Care. This is what happened:

> In September, equipped with desks, blackboard, books, pens – just like a real school – I proceeded to 'educate' my children. By the end of the day we were all verging on a nervous breakdown. The children had done no work. How could they? I had spent the day screaming at them! I knew it was all a mistake – how could I hope to come up to the standards set by 'them' when I was a mere parent – one of 'us' – no qualifications. By about two in the morning I had worked out the problem – I was trying to be a school. I was doing exactly what I objected to the school doing to my children!
>
> Next day, to the delight of the children, who were dreading a repeat of our first day, I got a picnic together. We dressed warmly and went off to walk across Tennyson Down for the day. We gathered flowers, a giant toadstool, feathers, shells, we spotted birds and insects and met lots of people, had conversations with them and generally had a lovely day. After the children went to bed I wrote in my EO record/diary (long-since abandoned) – Subjects covered today – physical exercise, history, nature, geography and socialization! For the rest of that week we drew pictures and wrote about our day out. Pressed the collected flowers, after identifying them, and stuck them on card on the walls/doors. We all decided that the second day was much preferred to the first but that we must make some effort to compromise

and get some work in books to present to the 'authorities'.

In two years of home education we have changed, evolved. We sold the blackboard and the desks as we did not like living in a classroom and hangman could be played on card instead of a blackboard anyway. We now devote more time to practical subjects and less to laborious writing in books. We cook, work on our old car and motorbike. We write poems (Matthew's speciality), write stories (Leila's favourite), read books, write letters, dig the garden (hoping to grow our own veg. and fruit this year), decorate the house, repair broken items, meet people, draw pictures, do jig-saws, play games, sing songs, listen to music. Of course we do maths and English, discuss history, look at maps, talk about the world, spin the globe, listen to the news, but again it's mainly practical work or discussion.

We have had no visits from any 'authority figures' for over a year now. For the first year we had visits each term from a fantastic education advisor who was so popular with my children that we used to have to bake a cake for his visit. He was greeted by a hug by my younger two – Leila and Danny running down the path to hug him. He was invited to birthday parties and got Easter and Christmas cards. He still has the 1984 card made by Leila hanging in his office!

With certain children there might need to be more than a period of transition. They sometimes need time to recover from being at school, so that they can find confidence in their abilities once more. Parents may find this time difficult. Perhaps they did not imagine that their children would continue to have problems once school had been left behind. A child may show strong resistance to working or learning, perhaps generally or perhaps in a specific area. The answer may be just to ease up, to let the child realize that the pressure she has been under is now off. It is hard to be patient, to be relaxed about something you do not really feel relaxed about – and this might be the case particularly if the problem is in an

area that you see as all-important. Skills like writing or reading
provide a foundation for so many other aspects of education
but trying to push a child on in the face of opposition may only
prolong the difficult time. In schools, children who fall behind
may never make up the lost ground but at home the situation is
quite different.

Leslie Downie describes how her son gradually overcame
his school-induced resistence to writing:

> Ewan is nearly ten and has been able to read well for some
> years. He has an insatiable appetite for a wide range of
> books and stories from *Tintin* to *The Lord of the Rings* and
> information books on almost every subject. When he
> came out of school at the age of seven he was really
> 'screwed up' about writing. After nine months, we were
> working abroad and he wanted to write home. He would
> sit down to copy his own words from my writing and I
> could see the tension mount in him. He would sit
> clenching the pencil and say, 'I can't do it. When I sit
> down to write I feel like I'm going to have to write and
> write and write like I had to at school.'
> So we would talk about his feelings and I would try to
> encourage him to do just a little and then we would leave
> off writing for months. His writing and spelling were
> awful and I can't pretend I wasn't worried but I kept
> telling myself that he would get there. At his request,
> over the past 18 months he has had occasional writing
> practice, typing and spelling, and once or twice he has
> spontaneously written notices for his room or angry
> notes to me, but I have refused to push him, feeling
> instinctively that it would set him back. Maturation is a
> large part of the process of gaining fine control of the
> fingers and I reassured myself that he did do other things
> with his hands. After a month of not writing, he
> surprised himself by being able to write much more
> easily with less physical effort. However he still lacked
> confidence to try on his own and I felt that he was
> self-critical of his own efforts. 'Is his ability to read
> inhibiting his writing?' I asked myself. 'Surely a child

who reads as he does must know what words look like and be able to recognize when a familiar word is wrongly spelt. Perhaps if he could gain confidence with spelling, confidence with writing would follow.'

So one day when he was making a poster on seal culling and asked me a word, I suggested he try the word in as many different ways as he could think of and pick the one that looked right to him. After six tries he delighted himself by finding the right one. From this small step forward we tried spelling by trial and error using Scrabble letters. This seemed less of a threat than writing words down. And now when he writes notices for a game, he is confident enough to guess at the spelling or to experiment on a scrap of paper to find the word he needs. Recently a notice appeared which said 'beware of the snake' and I found a scrap which said, 'snact snacke shacke snace snake'.

Ewan is now keen to learn to spell verbally and we have been working through a box of spelling cards I borrowed from the local Teachers' Centre. I feel he has impressed himself by getting through the cards with ease and at the same time (much to my relief) he is becoming relaxed about writing.

I feel we have made a breakthrough. With guesswork, guidance and trust, Ewan is overcoming his writing problem himself and feeling a sense of achievement as a result.

Here is another account of a family in this adjustment period. Rena Laslett writes about life with her children, Ninya, age eleven, and Jessica, nearly ten, after they were withdrawn from school:

When I think of how we start the day, I am reminded of the infant song, 'Each day different and every day new'. Some mornings are lazy and slow – all in one bed drinking tea – our wide-ranging dialogue may be serious or hilarious, sometimes we're peaceful, sometimes riotous. Other mornings, any one of us may be up, busy on something left the night before.

Ninya and Jessica both had a transitionary period when they were first at home. The pattern was the same: they thought that being out of school would be a doddle but, as they assumed responsibility for their own lives and learning, they both concluded that it was hard work. Worse than school? – no. Much, much better was their unanimous conclusion. This initial phase was like a recovery period. Five years in school had taught them to be passive consumers; the opportunity to take the reins now was not a little daunting.

The satisfaction that they get out of an activity or piece of work when they have been the controlling force in planning/implementation is quite clear, and my response to them has shifted accordingly – no need for lip service, 'That's nice dear'. I am genuinely impressed with their results (and I think their capabilities are still a surprise to them!)

Some days still fall apart (though these days occur much less frequently than at the beginning). We have learnt to ride them out and to laugh at ourselves afterwards. We have had to learn to live with one another again – I had been used to having hours to myself since they first went to school. Nevertheless, the feeling of rightness that we get from good days is really exciting. The difference, it seems now, is that they are no longer restricted to tinkering with the idea of living – they are living.

In the following account by Wendy Razzell, two main questions that bother many parents are explored. One is the dilemma that many of us feel about examinations – as Wendy describes:

Exams may seem to represent everything we have rejected about school-based education: rote-learning, competitiveness and learning from a set syllabus rather than from the felt needs and interests of the individual. On the other hand, not to do them is to opt more completely out of the system and possibly block paths to further education courses or work training.

The other is the worry about isolation, not only that the children will feel cut off from others but also that the adults' lives will become restricted and insular – and this is of particular concern in one-parent families where there is no other adult to share the load. By the time Wendy's children, Josephine and Luke, were in their early teens they had had alternating experiences of school and a 'running-free' variety of home education. When they were first withdrawn from school they went to live in a rural community where there were other deschooled children. They then lived as a one-parent nuclear family with the children back at school but:

> After the freedom from institutional life, the return to a school-orientated existence was claustrophobic and depressing to us all. It still seemed as if some kind of community would be the only suitable environment for us if we were going to deschool again. The image of us incestuously closeted together day after day in a small town house, in an area where all the other kids were at school just didn't seem feasible. And I had little idea what I'd 'do' with them on my own. But we did know that school wasn't right. Jos was feeling oppressed by the heavy secondary work load that left no time for her own interests and was very unhappy with school social life. Luke was uninspired by his primary school and was developing so many fears about the petty regulations, the non-observance of which was a heinous crime.

They again tried life in a rural community, living an extremely basic existence in a caravan in a remote spot without electricity or running water:

> It was a physical outdoor life, except for times when the winter gales blew for days on end. It wasn't a situation conducive to formal working, though Luke kept his hand in at maths and Jos started to work on three 'O' Level courses by correspondence. We read lots of books aloud to pass the long winter evenings and enjoyed the beautiful countryside. The children made camps and tree-houses, looked after the animals and started badminton, dancing and music lessons.

Wanting to avoid a second caravan winter, they moved again, this time to a house in another area that was rural but not remote. On this return from the wilds the children did not go back to school:

> Here we were, finally, in the situation that I'd been running away from for several years – just the children and myself in a house on our own, out of school, and in a totally unfamiliar part of the world into the bargain. And it's actually fine and all my previous doubts seem unfounded. In our small neighbourhood community there are four other families all with children at school or due to go but it isn't a problem at all. We've been completely accepted. We had a small trauma in the autumn when the L.E.A., after a short visit, wrote to say that they were not satisfied with the education being given. This has since been resolved after we explained in detail what we were doing and our reasons for it and I emphasized our shared commitment to carrying on.

The L.E.A. was concerned that Wendy, as a single parent, might not be able to 'keep going' for the necessary five years until Luke reached 16. They also expressed concern about the lack of facilities for science or computing. She assured them that if either of the children wanted to pursue these subjects, she would make sure they were able to do so. A home computer was bought; Luke showed interest and taught himself a great deal from books. But the L.E.A.'s attitude and expectations did present the family with a challenge to their way of life. They adopted a more definite structure, working regularly. Josephine worked hard on her 'O' Level correspondence courses. She was able to find out that she was capable of taking exams, something she had wondered about, and also discovered she could do well. Not being swamped by all the pressures of school, she still had plenty of time for her other interests, for music and crafts, patchwork, weaving, editing her own magazine and working with a group of 'special needs' children:

> We still debate how far we should be influenced by

society's exam mania, as we are quite strongly at present reinforced by the L.E.A.'s pressure on us to prove ourselves at least equal to school provision. We've had a sense of achievement at finding that we are quite capable of doing school-type work efficiently and enjoyably but there's still a strong sense of déjà-vu about the old school subjects. Learning French verbs doesn't have much to do with speaking to French people and you wonder just when knowing how to manipulate an inverse matrix is going to matter. But the marvellous thing about home education is the freedom to respond to these doubts and experiment with shifts in approach in a flexible way. In any event, there's no doubt that Jos and Luke are infinitely happier and livelier than they were at school. My fears of being very isolated and having no personal freedom haven't been borne out at all.

Here is another account of 'O' Levels out of school, written by Nick Everdell. This gives a student's view of tackling examinations:

By the time I left school, just before my thirteenth birthday, I had been convinced by the teachers that 'O' Levels were tremendously difficult and that I would only pass them by doing exactly what they told me to and working like a Trojan. It took me several months to get rid of this negative state of mind; only when I began correspondence courses in the seven subjects I wanted to take did I realize that they weren't so difficult after all.

I worked in the mornings only for much of the two years; each subject was divided up into a certain number of lessons; I worked out how often I needed to complete a lesson to get finished by the exam date. And so I had a 'timetable' of sorts; this was the only thing that determined how fast I worked.

Most of the subjects assumed no previous knowledge, the textbooks themselves are very clearly written and leave very little unsaid that is necessary.

Whenever I came across something I couldn't understand, the first thing I didn't do was panic, as I had often done at school. I would read through the work again; if it was something minor I might leave it for a fresh attempt later; if it was something major, and still not understood after several attempts, it always meant that I had not grasped what led up to it thoroughly enough, so it was simply a case of revising previous work.

All this might sound difficult – it was not; in fact, I rarely got stuck. This was not through any special ability of my own but simply because I did the work methodically, making sure I understood one thing before moving onto the next.

Above all, I worked in a relaxed environment with no outside pressures as in school. I discovered that a keenness to study developed that I'd never had through a traditional school education.

Science subjects require some practical work but I was careful to choose a syllabus that didn't set a practical exam. However, being at home, there were endless opportunities for simple experiments connected with the three sciences, biology especially. I grew a lemon tree and an oak tree, planted two seed potatoes, one with fertilizer and one without, to see how the crop from each compared. I developed a Cabbage White butterfly in captivity, from egg to adult.

For chemistry I obtained some of the more common chemicals from a chemists and did endless experiments; making hydrogen gas was one of the most worthwhile of these. The aim here was to get a toy balloon to float; I remember feeling a tremendous sense of achievement when I eventually managed this.

I sat the exams as an external candidate at the local technical college; this was a daunting prospect, as I was a total stranger to the place – however this was no problem, once I had sat down in the exam room. My preparation had been thorough enough (too thorough in some subjects) and I didn't find the papers too difficult. In fact, the exams were quite enjoyable and I felt a great sense of accomplishment.

Overall I can say that being deschooled was a definite turning point in my life – a transformation from misery to contentment and confidence; the 'O' Levels were almost a by-product of the experience; and I very much doubt if I would have passed any exams had I stayed in school.

Nick's method of study was not the forty-minute period structure that he had been accustomed to in school. When he needed to, he would spend days at a time on a topic.

When he was withdrawn from school – after two years of secondary schooling which had, as his mother described, reduced him to a shadow of his former confident self – his parents were told that leaving was, in itself, a failure. The family decided that he could work for his 'O' Levels at home but his father was assured by a representative of the L.E.A. that Nick was certain to fail. And this was a judgement from someone who had never even met Nick. His parents tried to remove any worries he had about failing by saying he could always re-sit any exams that he did not pass the first time or perhaps he could find employment that did not require qualifications.

In fact, Nick passed all seven at his first sitting – and was awarded grade A, top marks, in every subject. Even the L.E.A. sent him a letter of congratulation. He went on to study for 'A' Levels under a flexible arrangement with the local technical college whereby he did not have to attend many classes; so he was in effect still teaching himself. He then went on to King's College, Cambridge.

The message is certainly that being out of school does not limit you to only one sort of education. Unlike those at school, the possibilities are many and various. The few families mentioned in this chapter clearly show that there are many approaches to home education, each of them as successful as they are individual. Primary or secondary, free or formal – do it the way that suits your family best.

10

How Home Education has worked out for us

Although I certainly came to motherhood armed with theories about children and their upbringing, as it has turned out we don't adhere to any one theory or follow any particular method. We draw from one set of ideas or another as it suits us, adapting as we go along. The periods spent playing and talking with Hosanna and Fiorin when they were smaller gradually developed into sessions that had a more obvious learning element. There was no point when we suddenly switched on the education. It had been going on continuously since birth.

From this beginning it was a very gentle transition that led us, when Hosanna was about five or six, to start using the term 'schoolwork'. I had always spent time working with her and it was our intention to continue. Although we could perhaps have come up with a better name, 'schoolwork' did seem an honest one to us and she found it perfectly acceptable. She saw other children had to go to school, after all, and so she found it reasonable that she should do some work of a similar kind at home.

Children do not grow up in a vacuum. They learn from what they have around them and we influence that process whether we recognize it or not. We are, ourselves, a valuable resource. I do not entirely agree with Rousseau's maxim, 'Surround him with all the lessons you would have him learn without awaking his suspicions'. This makes it sound as if education is some sort of benign confidence trick. Surround her instead with your normal family life, and she will learn a great deal. It may be that she will pick up a complete education this way without recourse to other methods. However, this doesn't always happen. It may depend on what your idea of an adequate education is – which may be quite different from my idea. It will also depend on how skilful you are at providing the opportunities to learn. But I certainly did not want to be constantly manipulating the environment to achieve what I see as an education, apparently by chance.

Early on, Victor and I discussed the possibility of letting a child educate herself totally through her own explorations and discoveries. Rousseau suggests that before coming to use a microscope, the child should first invent it. It sounded a challenging idea and we gave it some thought. As we saw it though, it was an impossible task to expect of a child. She had only one lifetime whereas it took mankind innumerable lifetimes to discover how to make fire or invent the wheel, let alone find out that the earth goes round the sun or that radioactive fall-out is lethal. We are all heavily dependent on the discoveries of other people. Children can make many discoveries through play, yes, but they are not going to make it to the twentieth century without contact with existing ideas and knowledge.

We wanted to avoid over-burdening play with too much educational content. As Isaac Taylor wrote in his book, *Home Education*, over a century and a half ago, 'Let play be play and nothing else'. We did not want to be parents who were all the time on the look-out for a 'learning situation', ready to leap in with a carefully disguised lesson. If you think your child needs to learn maths, say, it seems to me you have several options. You can leave her to pick up what she can and hope that is adequate. Or you can look out for 'mathematical learning situations' and weave them into the play. Or you can let her get on and play what she wants, however unmathematical, and do some maths with her from time to time. My feeling is that the first option is leaving the matter to chance. You may be happy to. I may not. The second option is fine as long as you leave her plenty of room not to play maths if she doesn't want to and don't get into misunderstandings about her right to say, 'Enough of that now, thanks. I want to play horses.' The third option is roughly what we do: the child can play as she wants without our needing to wonder about the educational content. The 'schoolwork' works as a back-up system – what does not get picked up one way is covered, in time, another way.

Perhaps what I have said makes it sound as if we have formal lessons. In fact, they vary greatly. I believe that when Hosanna and Fiorin are older they will wish to be literate and numerate and that they will be better prepared for this if they practise their skills on a reasonably regular basis. But they don't need to spend most of their waking day doing it.

I have found that when we keep a note of the day's activities, it provides me with many surprises when I look back. It is easy to forget the conversations you have with your children or to think that very little learning is going on. Looking back over my work journals I get a completely different perspective. I see that from the earliest years we have done more maths than I would have remembered – very gently, not at all the pages of sums written in the workbook approach, but nevertheless covering a lot of ground. Here is an extract from my journal dated 15th October 1981 when Hosanna was just over five:

> I gave Hosanna a piece of paper with the number 1 on and asked her to make a set (of conkers, buttons or whatever she could find) to match the number. Then 2, then 3 – very straightforward up to 9. At 10 we talked about now having two digits. We tallied with our fingers. So 10 would match up to 1 set of fingers and 0 more. I pointed out the digits in 10, how this showed 1 set of 10 and no more. We talked about how people might have come to use a base of 10, because of tallying with fingers.
>
> Given a piece of paper with 11 on it, she immediately realized it was easiest to match the 11 cotton reels up to the 10 pens she had already laid out and then 1 more. Again discussed how this was shown by the digits in 11 and we also matched up the 1 left over with the set of 1 acorn laid out earlier.
>
> Very quickly H saw the connection and now when she was given 12, 13, 14 she could see that it was in each case 1 set of 10 and so many more, exactly corresponding to the sets of 2, 3, 4 she had laid out earlier. I then started to ask her what number I should write down next and how to write it.
>
> As we neared 20 I asked her to think what would happen now. She said we had 2 lots of 10 so we should write a number starting 2 not 1. She got quite excited when she saw that these would be followed by numbers starting 3, then 4, then 5 and that in each case they would have 0

more then 1 more, then 2 more, just as the first numbers had. She went right through to the 90s, using the sets we already had to show me what would come next. She was able to tell me how to write each number. She suddenly saw *why* numbers were written the way they were.

Simple as it was, this combined many important ideas about number, the place system, sets, one-to-one correspondence. I had not planned this lesson; it had come about quite casually. As we reached 100 she broke off and started to do some building with Cuisenaire rods (see page 186), thoughtfully as if assimilating what had gone before. A little later she asked me what a satellite was so we talked about man-made and natural satellites. This led us on to talking about the moon and its effects on the earth, how it acted like a magnet to cause tides.

After Fiorin was born there was another quite natural but essential development: Hosanna began to spend more time working by herself. At first a great deal of my day was taken up with the new baby but I was still available for talk and this was how most of the real education went on for a while.

Here is another extract from my journal, a partial account of Wednesday 6th April 1983 when Fiorin was a year old and Hosanna was six and a half:

A dictation. Hosanna then added more words to her word book. We talked about -i ending being Italian not English, then we talked about -y ending: by, my, shy, try compared to pony, happy, baby etc.

H did Aboriginal finger counting (based on the binary number system which has only two digits, 1 and 0, i.e. a base of two.) She enjoys having skills that other people might be baffled by, being able to count to over a thousand just on her fingers! She then 'translated' numbers into binary notation, using her fingers to work it out.

Long conversation about Quakers and how their beliefs differ from mainstream Christianity. This came about because of Hosanna's question about the name on the porridge packet. I talked about pacifism and the Quakers' emphasis on the inward rather than the outward forms of religion. This led us on to Roman Catholics. H was concerned if a certain Catholic family we knew were aware that we weren't Catholics. Would they still like us if they knew? We talked about religious tolerance and wishing to convert others – which led us on to Jehovah's Witnesses and evangelism.

After a pause H brought up the subject of Heaven and Hell. Did I believe in it? Did she? We talked about behaving well rather than religiously. Which did she think was more important – being kind and considerate or going to church?

Later talked about genes. H clearly very interested in subject and kept returning to it throughout the day. She said she loved the idea of genes – it seemed so mysterious and marvellous. Talked about mothers' and fathers' genes, test-tube babies, heredity, nature or nurture deciding people's non-physical characteristics, natural cloning – in aphids for example – and possibilities of artifical cloning. She asked whether it was possible to mix genes, other than by a sperm fertilizing an egg. Talked about genetic engineering, discussion of relative sizes of eggs –human compared to hen's or frog's egg.

H did some drawing with compasses. Later with gold ink. Lettering. Talked about illuminated manuscripts, books before the days of printing, why printworkers call their union meetings chapel meetings and their union official the F.O.C. (Father of Chapel) – a legacy from the days when books were made by monks. I told her about the description of the coming of the printing press in the novel I was reading, *The Cloister and the Hearth*, and we talked about the effect this might have on the calligraphers of the time.

And so on – this was just part of the day's conversations and is typical of so many entries in the journal. The direction the talk flowed in was largely decided by Hosanna. If more questions were asked, the conversation went on. If different things were brought up, we might go off in another direction. If she went off to do something else, the matter was considered closed unless she took it up again later. On other days we would range far and wide on other topics. Looking back I see that religion and science were subjects that cropped up again and again. It can be seen from this that lessons – apart from her dictation and spelling Hosanna did other work that day, including some time-telling practice and multiplication – pale into insignificance beside the rich and varied education that goes on at home.

We found that things worked out best when we had regular periods when we could talk or work together without feeling under pressure from outside commitments. Although I am pleased there are clubs and classes available, we have made very little use of such facilities ourselves. From our socially active beginning with different mornings and afternoons of the week allocated to specific activities, we have now settled into a pattern where very little of our week is organized. Over the years, at different times, Hosanna has been to classes in ballet, gymnastics, pottery and woodwork. Until she was nine or ten she went to Brownies. She is now a member of the Woodcraft Folk. From time to time there have been riding lessons. This is not exactly a full social calendar, being at most one or two evenings or afternoons a week. I take the view that if I were to spend my day shunting my children about from one class or event to another, they could just as well be at school. We see home education as being family based, not as something where individual members are always splintering off doing organized peer group activities.

Perhaps I am fortunate in having naturally out-going and sociable daughters. We are certainly fortunate in living in an area well provided with green spaces where they can play with the local children. We also have a couple of other families with children out of school living very near to us, as well as several others a little further afield. Isolation has never been a problem for us.

One day recently at bedtime, when Hosanna was being asked to clear away her things from the garden and come in, there were – typically – clusters of children lingering at the side gate, in the garden and on the front lawn. While absent-mindedly gathering up all her stuff, she circulated from one group to the next, loitering and chatting. As we waited with growing impatience, Victor remarked to me in exasperation, 'You can rely on Hosanna to turn anything into a social event!' which sums it up.

Like anyone else, we have our bad days when everything gets off to a wrong start and stays that way. Here is a note that I kept of such a day. Fiorin was not yet three and Hosanna was eight plus. Fiorin had been ill and had not quite recovered, so was not at all her usual self. The children may not have been behaving very well but, as I realized later, nor was I. I had decided it was high time Hosanna took to practising the recorder regularly – and I grimly decided to enforce this:

Monday 19th November 1984

H played slowly, badly, tunelessly, expressionlessly, the wrong notes at the wrong pace, stamping and wriggling all the while, even berating and blaming the recorder. She had not played a single tune properly. Every time I turned my back, she stopped playing. Every time I left the room she put the recorder down and slid off to do something else. Finally, I told her that if she wasn't prepared to practise now, she should put her recorder away and do it later – instead of going out to play.

F meanwhile had played with dough, then with water. I read with her. F drew, then tipped toys all over the floor. F started squashing the dog, and putting things on the cat who was trying to sleep. F started throwing things around, H annoying F to orchestrate things. Dog kept accosting F, inviting her to fresh assault. I maundered around in the wake of it all, issuing threats, nagging, tidying up, physically pulling child from child, child from beast. I went off to clean the windows. Fiorin abandoned the dog and cat and clung to me, moaning. I felt I had been trying to wade through glue all day.

I recorded a piece of Bach from the radio. When I replayed it I found that at the end of the tape there was an unintended piece of recording–

H (on tape recorder): How do wild sheep shear themselves?

Me (a pause – my thoughts are elsewhere) . . . um . . .

They don't. . . .
H: Well, how do they get on in summer?
Me: (Pause) . . . They . . . um . . . have long coats . . .
They get hot. . . .
Hearing this was quite a shock. I hadn't realized how limp I was being. Nevertheless, later I decided it was time for that recorder practice. H played the tunes that she had played so badly this morning fully as badly this afternoon. I gave her a demonstration, playing her the tunes myself – how pleasant they sounded! How painful it was to get her to play them! Does one give up or march her on? (Isn't music meant to be enjoyed?)

Clearly I had forgotten my own experience of music lessons at school!

H bargained to do some sums in a workbook (!) instead and I agreed. She asked if she could go out when she had finished them. I looked at the page, saw there was a lot to do and agreed she could: it didn't seem like an easy way out. She promptly did 48 sums in about ten minutes and went off to play . . . singing.

Another entry in the same month gives a different picture:

H continued writing her account of the *Odyssey*. I am astounded at her ability to produce suitably courtly language. The noblemen converse with each other with lordly grandeur. (Later when she took this to Brownies as part of the material for her Writer's badge, the tester didn't realize it was her own composition and presumed she had copied it verbatim from a book – as did Victor when he read it.)
Went on walk to Beckford's Tower through the back lanes up through Lansdown. Passed Winifred's Well Cottage. Talked about the Leaden Echo and the Golden Echo. Talked about the sun symbol on the walls of old houses. Discovered we had aimed for the wrong tower so had to walk on. Went into the cemetery through the gate inscribed 'Gate of Death' and tried to come out through 'Resurgent' but found it was locked. Beckford's

Tower had just closed for the Winter. Dusk fell as we stood in the gloomy porchway, disappointed and talking about the feeling we all had of dark spirits. Walked back to town. Met Patrick on the way. When he heard where we had been, told us of Beckford's involvement with black magic. Children greatly interested.

Hosanna is nearly eleven and has learned at home the skills she would have learned in infant and junior schools and, I believe, a lot more besides. She has always been a willing learner – very interested to listen, to talk, to read, to experiment, to imagine, to create – but not always the most industrious of workers. I don't believe this has anything to do with never having been to school. She works in spurts and surges. As a toddler she seldom showed the workmanlike devotion to repetitive work that Montessori observed in the very young and still less the desire for order that is supposed to characterize that age. A friend once said of Hosanna when she was little that she was not closely attached to the earth – she often felt she might suddenly fly away. It sounds funny but I know exactly what she meant. You only have to look at the way she moves to see this sort of lightness, the lack of plod, that is reflected in her mental agility.

She loves reading and will get through a couple of novels in an evening. Her favourite books reflect her love of animals and outdoor adventures. Arthur Ransome's *Swallows and Amazons* series, Jack London's two books *White Fang* and *The Call of the Wild*, Richard Adams's *Watership Down* and Henry Williamson's *Tarka the Otter* are all enduring favourites. Most recently she has enjoyed *Macbeth* and *Jane Eyre* as well as books by Gerald Durrell and Ursula Le Guin. She likes poetry – reading, hearing and composing it. I have paused here to ask her what poems she likes and she has mentioned, among others, several by such poets as Blake, Tennyson, Wordsworth, C. Day Lewis, Yeats and Hughes. Her own poetry is unlike any other children's poetry that I have read.

Perhaps more surprising to me, though, is to find myself the mother of a child as athletic as Hosanna. In that respect she is very different from me but then she has never been compelled to participate in sport or organized games at school. She has a great deal of physical stamina and loves running, jumping and climbing. Her great love is riding which, alas for her, we are unable to afford very often.

One day when she was six she decided to run round the running track of the local secondary school's playing field. Victor joined her for one lap and I joined her for another but she not only ran faster than us both but just kept on running. After the first couple of laps, we begged her to stop, thinking that perhaps young children should not run long distances. She completed five laps, all on the outermost, longest track, a considerable distance. When she was a very young child we awarded her the title 'Champion Walker' which she well deserved. Even when she was three or four she would return from long walks still with energy to run off though she had skipped to and fro all along the way. I recount this not because it is especially remarkable but to show that home educated kids are by no means wilting violets or stop-at-home swots.

As far as 'schoolwork' goes, she has tended to find workbooks rather dull, unlike Fiorin who, from an early age, saw them as some sort of emblem of the privilege of being old enough to do 'real work'. We have steered clear of them generally except in maths where we felt we needed a graded scheme to use as a back-up to the other work we were doing. We have used them less and less over the years. I remember reading somewhere that children often draw beautifully until they encounter workbooks. They then start turning out quick sketchy symbols similar to those in the illustrations they see – they no longer imagine for themselves how to draw a nose, they no longer look carefully at faces, but copy the blob or triangle that represents a nose in the workbooks. Betty Edwards, in her book *Drawing on the Right Side of the Brain*, also sees this grasping for a quick easy symbol as one of the reasons why many adults and older children draw so badly.

Hosanna's favourite subjects, she says, are chemistry and Latin, both of which were started when she was nine, at her request. I can see why she enjoys doing chemistry experiments but Latin might seem an unusual choice. I think she likes it because she sees the codelike aspect of it, a language that no one speaks and few people understand. She finds the idea of deciphering a sentence and discovering the hidden meaning – or of translating a sentence from English into this semi-secret language – quite fascinating. I thought this interest might wane once she realized there were sundry conjugations and declensions to come to grips with – she was never particularly keen on anything as dull as learning by rote – but she is as keen as ever.

Here is an account of Saturday 5th July 1986, soon after Hosanna's tenth birthday when she had received an electronics set:

> Walk along old railway bank, picked twigs to identify. H and F drew birds and talked about them at breakfast. They then drew twigs. Fed and cleaned out rabbits.
>
> V and H read chapter on the Great Wall of China from the old Wonders of the Ancient World books. Looked at the old photographs. Read Borges's essay 'The Wall and the Books'. Looked up Wall in the atlas.
>
> H keen to do more electronics and decided to make a transistor radio. Eager to do it alone so Victor left her to it. Wires right across the kitchen, to the tap for earth and through the window to the washing line for an aerial. Showed great care on wiring. Very clear reception. H proud and a bit amazed after the whisper from the crystal set. I came back from shopping, unsuspecting, and was greeted by a demonstration – the news on H's radio, clearer than on our own.

Meanwhile Fiorin is now five and has reached official school age. One morning recently I was awakened by her asking me, 'I like playing, but do you know what I like best?' 'No,' I said, 'What do you like best?' 'Schoolwork,' was her answer but she added, 'But you don't give me very much!' Perhaps this is a feature of being a second child in a house where the older one learns at home. The first may have had more individual attention, but the second is determined to keep up and try and do what the other is doing, however much work is involved. Having the example of an older sister to follow, Fiorin has insisted on being given 'schoolwork' too at times over the past couple of years. I take my lead very much from her, usually working with her at her invitation.

The interesting thing about Fiorin's keenness for work, I find, is the way that we have trailed behind her rather than led her. This wasn't wholly intentional but rather the result of my being busy on this book. However, we find that, with very little conscious teaching, she picks things up and demands to be shown more. The best example of this is her interest in writing. She will ask, 'How do you spell, 'The north wind doth blow and we shall have snow, and what will the robin do then, poor thing'' . . ?' and through she goes, carefully writing it all down as someone spells it out to her. In the mornings sometimes I wake to hear Hosanna sleepily giving her spellings. One day recently I made her bed and found a poster she had made – 'Don't kill rabbits. It is mean' – complete with drawings and then another little drawing of a horse marked 'Black Bess'. Last summer at a play-scheme in the local park she – the youngest there – was the only one seriously writing away, asking the organizer for spellings.

We have sometimes thought that Fiorin may be 'missing out' on some of the things I used to do with Hosanna. Apart from having less time now, I feel less inclined to get involved with the group activities that I no longer see as essential to a child's socialization. We have never bothered with playgroup for Fiorin. The only difference I notice is that she has had far fewer colds than her sister had when she was younger.

Perhaps what a second or later child loses in direct attention from the adult, she gains in indirect stimulation. I find it interesting that Fiorin has passed her 'landmarks' at almost exactly the same ages as Hosanna had. As a baby she was equally fast at getting mobile, walking sturdily from the day she was nine months old. Then in drawing and beginning to write and read, she made the same advances as Hosanna had about the same age, without the supposed stimulation of toddler group, playgroup or nursery school. I think back to that nursery school Hosanna went to: could it be that Fiorin is so eager and interested because she has never been led and has found her own way?

At certain stages, she has seldom been without pens, pencils or a pair of scissors in her hands, always busy drawing and cutting. For a month or two leading up to the Christmas before her fourth birthday she wrapped virtually anything she could lay hands on. If I wanted my pen, that was wrapped – a comb, that was wrapped – a paper clip, that was wrapped. She even reached the stage where she would wrap up the scissors and the sellotape. We had to develop the habit of looking inside any paper we found on the floor in case we were throwing away some carefully wrapped 'present'.

Perhaps in the future I will look back and remember Fiorin most of all with her suitcase – a child-size version of an old-fashioned case like a tiny evacuee in the War might have had. She carries around in it her pencils and equipment along with her baby seals and lamb tucked up in a small basket. This goes to bed with her at night. She wakes up before everyone else in the morning and, getting her suitcase out, busily carries on with her plans.

Fiorin mixes with other children without any problems. Having an older sister to keep an eye on her, she does have more freedom to play with a mix of local children on the green. There seems to be less need now for the swaps with other mothers though we still have children to stay, or play for the afternoon, but on a less organized basis and my two go off to visit other families regularly.

What we 'do' has been decided less by what we think the children ought to be learning at each stage and more by what interests us all. Neither of them are ever bored, as are so many children who are accustomed to the structure and organization of school. There is none of this 'What can we do? It's boring' approach to life. They always have a very good idea of exactly what they want to do without anyone telling them. They may ask us for materials, help, or advice but never for entertainment or ideas. Other parents I know with children who learn at home have also commented on this about their own families.

When Hosanna was younger we discovered the programmes for schools on television but we seldom watch them now, for three main reasons. The first was because I found that if we started the day with the children in front of the television set, we were more likely to find ourselves with limp children who would watch all day and do little else. Whatever educational benefit was gained from these programmes was more than offset by the effect of passively watching rather than actively doing. The second was that we found a week planned around various television programmes that we had to stay in to watch did not suit us at all.

The third reason was the way children's programmes are pitched. There seems to be the idea that a child won't watch anything, or learn anything, unless it is entertaining – relentlessly entertaining is the expression that comes to mind. I notice a tendency to have not one presenter but two so that each has only a short snippet to say and the camera can flick to and fro between the two. Does a child really get bored if one person says more than half a dozen sentences at a time? I suppose they soon will if this is all that is expected of them. In some programmes jingles and 'computer' sounds are sprinkled around ad nauseam. It is the opposite extreme from learning through activity and conversation. Television has its limitations as well as its possibilities.

But yes, my children do watch television sometimes – towards the end of the day, perhaps more often in winter, but not a great deal.

Our approach to home education is far from being a shining example, as we are well aware. We have sometimes wondered if we would not go back and do it all differently if we had the chance. At times I have felt I should have been indefatigable and given my children a more structured training in infancy. I suppose I am particularly prone to this state of mind when I read books about incredibly talented toddlers. It is all too easy to feel as if you have missed the boat, but for me this sort of regret is fairly short-lived. Small children have a lot to learn and if we are constantly teaching or training them, directing their attention here or there, they can miss out on those valuable things that they can only learn for themselves. At other times I feel it would have been marvellous to have thrown all lessons out of the window and instead to have concentrated wholly on the Poetic Spirit.

But if we were to go back and do it again – well, we still would not send the children to school. I am not going to pretend that we never have a moment's doubt about what we are doing but, on the whole, it seems right. I admit it can sometimes seem arduous having children at home all the time. There are moments when there seems so much to do that school seems like a very easy alternative. Why do it the hard way when there are teachers ready to do the job of looking after them for you? But, standing in a supermarket queue and listening to the things some women have to say about the horrors of the school holidays ('Can't wait for next Monday!'), I realize that school does not solve problems but just gives you less time to come to grips with them. Other parents find their children tiresome in small doses. Perhaps the problems of life with very young people become more concentrated when you spend less time with them.

I feel it is important not to let your respect for your children's rights swamp your own rights. I do not think that each generation must sacrifice itself slavishly for the next. We think there are times when children ought to get on and do what has to be done, whatever that is. Having them at home does depend on their willingness to function without us running around after them constantly. I could not look to the future and feel that home education was going to be a success if I thought that we would have to carry them through on our backs. The aim of good parents is the same as the aim of good educators: gradually to make themselves redundant.

I started off by outlining my early view of home education – children reared in a rural environment, isolated from the mediocre, offered only the finest sustenance 'to nourish dreams'. In reality I have not (yet) achieved my rural idyll and have compromised to a far greater extent than I, at 16, would have imagined. If I were able to go back and start all over again. . . . I hope I would compromise a little less. Would I throw out the telly? Yes, I think I should.

And would I throw out the toys? We noticed from very early on, apart from one or two soft toy 'pets' (the enduring favourites, Snowy and Sea the seals, made at home, incidentally), the most prized possessions in our house are in fact sticks, cardboard boxes and pieces of rope. My children do play with toys – little people and dolls house furniture arranged on a bookshelf or window-sill, miniature farm animals and a Beware of the Bull sign on the flower-bed – but I can't really see that they have been corrupted by them or are any less imaginative because of them. But yes, I suppose, if I were to go back I would dispense with a lot of the other toys they have accumulated. I recall a friend of mine once saying, 'Toys are only a substitute for the "Great Outdoors" – parents only give them to their children to compensate for a lack of parental attention.' I am inclined to agree with him to a certain extent.

Things have moved on even in the months that I have been writing this book. Perhaps because I have been spending time doing something else, I can look at my children and see they are growing up fast. Fiorin could have started school by now and has made the transition to girlhood very suddenly. Hosanna is long-legged and looks ready to shoot into adolescence before too long. I feel we are about to move into another new phase. Victor sees the secondary-school years as an important challenge. We tend to look back and see that we have come a long way in the past five years or so. I see no reason why we should not make equally dramatic progress over the next few years. When examinations seem appropriate I feel we will be able to cope with them.

Our most recent visit from the L.E.A. Advisor came after a period without any regular 'schoolwork'. We had decided to enjoy the summer out of doors. Just as we were thinking of reinstating something like lessons, Hosanna caught glandular fever which made her unwell for a surprisingly long time. Then came the letter announcing the impending visit. I admit I did feel some trepidation at having rather little to 'show' compared with earlier visits. However all went very well.

The Advisor, who had originally seemed quite hostile to the idea of home education, had become warmer and more sympathetic with each visit. And this was no exception. By now, she was demonstrably impressed with the results. In this atmosphere, I felt able to mention that it was a great pity to feel under pressure to produce 'evidence' that education was going on: children learn without always having the need for formal lessons and written recording. She was quick to agree and pointed out that teachers feel under the same pressure from parents who like to see exercise books full of neat work. That was not at all what education was about, she said. Children might learn a great deal and yet produce very little written evidence in the process. I was very pleased to hear this from an L.E.A. Advisor.

Our visit was friendly and relaxed. Fiorin, concerned to establish that she, too, was being home educated, was particularly eager to show her work. They had both clearly made a great deal of progress since the Advisor had last seen them and her parting words to us all were 'Keep up the good work'!

Home education, as I see it, is not about producing prodigies or nurturing precocious talents. There is no hot-house development of geniuses going on in any of the households I know. If, in the course of trying to show that learning at home can be successful, I have given the impression of special intelligence or ability, then that is a pity – but perhaps inevitable. Looking at all the home-educated children we know, I see they are a mixed bunch generally, perhaps happier than average, certainly more confident, less crushed than those at school, maybe more lively or imaginative, capable or independent, perhaps more interested and caring, but they are as ordinary children should be.

When I think of home education compared to school, I often think of a sentence from Sylvia Ashton-Warner's book, *Myself*. The book isn't about home education (though, coincidentally, she was home educated until the age of eleven) but about having the courage to do what you feel is right even if it means daring to be different. One sentence captures the essence of the book–

> I must not avoid walking upright and with grace just because round-shouldered getting along is the order of the day.

Isn't round-shouldered getting along exactly what school is for many people? I am thinking of adults as well as children:

whole families can be liberated. It takes a bit of courage at first but it soon feels right. Yes, let us not be afraid to walk upright and with grace – even if everyone else's head is so far down we sometimes feel we are walking alone. We can see the world so much better this way. We can look around as we walk. We can look to the furthest horizon. Our step lightens. We may even find the children want to start running ahead.

Appendix I

A History of Home Education

Schools have been around for a long time but throughout most of history, the majority of children have had to get through life without them. Some people, I know, would argue that children managed perfectly well without schools and that the advent of compulsory education has been an imposition which has largely destroyed what they see as a more natural way of life.

Personally, I do not take that line. I can see that free and compulsory education for all played a vital role in bringing people to accept that children were not to be used as cheap labour. It helped to bring about our modern view that learning not labour is the proper business of childhood. State schools have not just been odious institutions for the daily incarceration of children. For all their faults – and they have many – their role in altering society's perception of the work expected of children should be acknowledged.

There is the argument used by some who oppose schools that, in former times, when children were free to work and to contribute to the family income, they gained a feeling of dignity and worth which modern dependence denies them. However, when children are free to labour they are also open to exploitation. I cannot see the sense in arguing for a return to a situation where children were 'free' to work in coal mines or factories. I am not even going to eulogize about the joys of children being able to help to bring in the harvest – I am sure it was hard work with little to be joyous about. Before the days when children – all children, not just those whose parents could afford the fees – were expected to be in school, the children of the poor often worked long hours for low wages in harsh conditions in industry and agriculture. Even today, in countries where education is not the accepted right of children, there is child labour. And where there is child labour, exploitation is rife.

If what Illich says of the past is true – 'The worker's child, the peasant's child and the nobleman's child all dressed the way their fathers dressed, played the way their fathers played and were hanged by the neck as were their fathers. After the discovery of "childhood" by the bourgeoisie all this changed,' (*Deschooling Society*) – then the change seems no bad thing. Childhood as we know it may have been an invention of the bourgeoisie, as he suggests, but I think it was one of their better ideas.

It is difficult to get a clear view of childhood in the past. Reading Lloyd de Mause's disturbing and depressing book, *The History of*

Childhood, I see that he, like Illich, believes that the perception of childhood prevalent today came about only very recently. Illich writes, 'The school system is a modern phenomenon, as is the childhood it produces,' but he sees modern childhood as 'a burden' which 'most people around the world . . . either do not want or cannot get'. De Mause takes the opposite stand to Illich. He suggests that childhood in the past was a dark world of exploitation and cruelty and that it is only since the middle of this century that we are beginning to get our attitudes to children right.

When I set about writing this account, I was aware of works by researchers like de Mause which give such a grim picture of children's lives throughout history. I was also wary of accepting the pleasant myth that there was greater freedom for all children in the days before compulsory education filled the classrooms. In considering how I could steer a course between the two extremes, I wondered how our own times would appear in comparison. If a future researcher were to go through the newspaper and court reports of today, she could assemble an appalling catalogue of evidence about the lives of children in Britain now – accounts of neglect, assault and murder, of a world where children are taught not to trust adults they don't know and where even parents brutally ill-treat their young. But it would be a distorted image: while the individual reports that make up this picture are true, the majority of children are brought up by well-meaning parents who try to give their children the care and consideration they need. I felt sure there were also caring parents throughout history.

Dr Linda Pollock in her book, *Forgotten Children*, sets out to re-examine recent theories about childhood. Through analysis of hundreds of English and American diaries and autobiographies dated from 1500 to 1900, she finds a more humane picture of parent–child relations. She concludes that there was a great deal of variation in parental care in the past (as there clearly is now). Mothers and fathers sat up at night to nurse sick children, wondered what to do for the best about education and had arguments with their offspring – and sometimes lost them – just as many do now.

No one can know how accurate anybody's picture of the past is, but Dr Pollock's view seems to me to be a balanced one. She drew from first-hand accounts – by parents and children – rather than the secondary sources often used by researchers (sermons, the writings of contemporary 'experts', newspaper reports and so on). It was with this view that I began looking for accounts of children learning at home in the past – and the accounts I found bore it out. There was a wide variation: some parents were dogmatic and harsh, others were flexible and caring.

I also realized, though, that just like secondary sources of information, primary sources are not necessarily wholly accurate. What are we to make of (home-educated) John Ruskin's well-known claim that he had no toys as a child apart from a bunch of keys? He said that the lack of amusements accounted for his absorption in patterns – in carpets, the wood of the floorboards, the bricks in a wall. In his autobiography, he agrees a cart, a ball and some wooden bricks were later added. The very first biography of Ruskin that I looked at said this was not true, that he was not especially deprived and even had a pet pony of his own. People have always like generating apocryphal stories about their childhood.

A number of the three hundred 'geniuses' or eminent persons studied by Dr Catherine Morris Cox in her book, *Genetic Studies of Genius, Volume Two – The Early Mental Traits of Three Hundred Geniuses*, did not go to school or went to school for only a short period of their childhood. A significant number were educated at home by parents, grandparents, aunts and sisters – or themselves. The picture that emerges is very different from the eleven years of compulsory schooling that is the norm today.

The details of those who went to school show us how institutions in the past – just as today – have failed to recognize qualities that did not fit into the accepted mould. Parents of late developers can take heart from examples like the writer, Oliver Goldsmith, who was schooled from the age of three. 'Never was so dull a boy,' said the mistress at his first school, 'he seemed impenetrably stupid.' At a later school he was considered a 'stupid, heavy blockhead, little better than a fool, whom everybody made fun of.' However his sister noted 'signs of genius' in him when he was very young. As a child, he would sit by the fire scribbling verses on scraps of paper which he would throw into the flames.

Or there was John Hunter, the noted surgeon and anatomist, who made little progress at school and was said to have been 'impenetrable to everything in the form of book-learning'. He learned to read late and with difficulty. 'John was good at games and an observer of nature from his earliest years; he had an aversion to books but he wanted to know all about the clouds and grasses, and why the leaves changed colour in the autumn. He watched the ants, bees, birds, tadpoles, and caddis worms, and he pestered people with questions about seemingly trivial things. At a very early age his interests were clearly defined and he would do nothing but what he liked.' It wasn't until he was twenty that he 'suddenly awoke from the indifference that had characterized him up to that time' and began to throw himself into working long hours towards his career.

The poet Thomas Chatterton was sent to school at the age of five but was soon returned home by the master 'as a confirmed dullard'.

After two years at home with his mother who taught him to read and write – which he learned with apparent difficulty – he returned to school. This 'confirmed dullard' had poetry published when he was ten years old and during the remaining seven years of his very short life produced a remarkable number of works – some of which he passed off as having been written in earlier centuries – which are now considered to show genius.

When Thomas Edison made little progress at school, his mother went to see the teacher to find out why, only to be told that the boy was 'addled'. Furious, she took him out of school and afterwards taught him at home herself. Before he died he had patented nearly 1300 inventions, a number never matched by any other inventor.

Jean de la Fontaine, the writer of fables, became interested in animals as a boy accompanying his father, a Commissioner of Waters and Forests, on his daily rounds. He loved wandering alone and 'found a melancholy happiness in idling away his time'. When he was first sent to school at the age of 14 he disliked both school and schoolwork. His teachers tried to force him to be like the other boys but found that no amount of discipline would make him fit the mould. They concluded he was a 'well disposed but hopeless dunce'.

Looking at the early biographical details of people in the past who became famous, it is difficult to see what they had in common. Some were extremely industrious and interested in academic study while others liked nothing better than to dream, to idle time away or to roam the fields or streets. Some were clearly gifted at a young age while others showed little sign of their latent abilities. No stereotype picture of childhood emerges: some hardly seemed to have had any childhood while others clearly had a carefree and happy time.

Some disliked school intensely – would they today be labelled 'school refusers'? Dumas, senior, the novelist, was an omnivorous reader from a very early age but was idle and disinterested in study, preferring the outdoor life. He had the run of the forest around the hamlet in which he lived. At the age of ten he was to be sent to school but managed to dissuade his mother from sending him by running away for a few days. He was allowed to continue to stay at home and had a few lessons a week instead from a local priest and teacher.

Lamartine, the French poet, was first sent to school at the age of eleven. He was made so miserable by the restrictions and brutality that he ran away from school and contemplated suicide. During his early years at home his parents had educated him by their own example. They had read Voltaire and Racine to him as he went off to sleep at night. They read and wrote in his company so that he would ask for their help in order to learn to do as they did.

Nathaniel Hawthorne, the American writer, went to school only 'half as much as other boys' and amused himself at home – doing such things as knitting socks for the cat. Although a lively child who enjoyed running wild in the woods near his home, during the middle years of his boyhood he was unable to walk because of a very protracted illness. He would read all day in silence – at the age of six, *Pilgrim's Progress* (then his favourite book) and a few years later Shakespeare, Milton, Spensers's *Faerie Queene*, Pope's *Iliad*, all before he was twelve. His lessons at home were irregular but his family was one where books and literature were part of daily life. Even when able to attend school, he had 'a grievous disinclination to go'.

Tennyson went to school between the ages of seven and eleven but loathed it. Taught at home by his father – two of his brothers also became notable poets – he, like Hawthorne, was keenly interested in animals as well as reading. The family acted out plays and wrote stories to read aloud to each other. Being unconventional and absorbed in their interests, they were considered very odd by the neighbours.

Some of these famous people were largely self-educated. Others may have received regular tuition – at home or at school – but it was what they did on their own which led to their later achievements.

James Watt, the inventor, was unable to go to school regularly because of poor health. As early as six, he would draw mathematical figures on the hearth as part of his private calculations. Using his set of tools, he would take his toys to pieces, inventing new ones. At school the other boys thought him mentally dull. At home, while sitting for hours watching the steam coming from the kettle, he would hold various objects over it to see the effect the steam had on them – on one occasion, to the exasperation of an aunt who thought he was wasting time.

Pascal, the French Philosopher and mathematician, never went to school and was taught by his father. Even when very young, he was consumed with curiosity, wanting to know the reasons for everything. He was not content until he felt he had logical answers and if he could not get them from other people he would devise his own. His sister said of him that he never gave up until he found a satisfactory explanation.

When his father decided that he was not ready to learn mathematics and deliberately put away all maths textbooks, the boy set about inventing his own geometry. Using charcoal he worked out ways to construct figures which he drew on his playroom walls. Not knowing the correct terms, he made up words of his own as he went along, calling circles 'rounds' and lines 'bars'. Pursuing answers to the questions these figures raised, he developed his own propositions and worked out ways to demonstrate them. This was before he was twelve years old.

Others received a rigorous training. John Wesley's mother gave her children formal teaching for six hours a day from the age of five. Their tuition was careful and strict, following a plan so that nothing was ever left until it was learned perfectly. Each lesson was repeated once, and often twice, later in the day. They made rapid progress and, when Wesley went to school at the age of eleven, he was an outstanding scholar. Perhaps his early training accounts for his tirelessness as an adult. Apart from his unparalleled achievement of delivering 40,000 sermons, covering 250,000 miles on horseback, his literary output was astonishing. Just reading the list of his published works did cause me an hour or two's thought about my whole view of education!

But the example of John Stuart Mill puts intensive training into a different light. He received a rigorous education almost from birth from his father, the philosopher James Mill. He was kept apart from other children and, as he himself said, he 'never was a boy'. The nearest he came to recreation was on the long walks that he went on with his father but, as much as anything else, these were occasions for lessons and oral examinations. His attention was always focused on the abstract and, as a result of this, he tended to be unaware of what was going on around him. At the age of three he began to study Greek and had to report to his father every day about his reading of the classics and history. By seven he was reading Plato. Among the other subjects he was taught by his father were Latin, mathematics, astronomy, philosophy, and political economy.

Although his studies were started at an extremely early age, complete understanding was aimed at before he was led to the next stage. Never hearing himself praised and having no one of his own age to measure himself against, he compared himself with his father. Consequently he was aware of his own ignorance rather than his intelligence and precocious ability. His father's friends treated him as their intellectual equal from his earliest years.

When he was fourteen he was sent to France to continue his education where he is said to have devoted nine hours a day to intensive intellectual labour as well as reading, driving, sight-seeing, swimming, collecting plants and insects, learning to sing, dance, fence and ride! At the age of twenty, already recognized as an influential thinker, he went through a period of depression which he attributed in part to his intensive education.

Two men whose education I will look at in a little more detail are Rousseau and Cobbett, both of whom wrote about their views on education at home. I include some description of their theories.

Jean Jacques Rousseau

As an infant, Rousseau was not expected to survive. His mother had died at his birth and so it was left to his father to bring him up. At a very early age he learned to read, apparently by himself. Subsequently, he and his father would sit up at night reading through a collection of romances, sometimes so absorbed that they might stay up all night to finish a book. At the age of seven, the boy turned to history. While his father worked, repairing watches, Jean Jacques would read aloud to him such works as Plutarch's *Lives*.

When he was ten, his father had to leave Geneva, following a brawl, and he was sent to live with relatives. With his cousin, he was taught at a pastor's house where he learned, as he said, 'insignificant twaddle'. At home with his father, reading had not been compulsory so he had devoted himself to it. Now that it was, he turned instead to manual activities. After a couple of years he and his cousin were taught drawing and geometry at his uncle's house but they were mostly left to themselves. They spent their days colouring and painting, trying to make watches and constructing models and instruments.

During his early teens he was said to have acted like a dunce. His first employer, a notary, found him utterly incompetent as a clerk and so dismissed him. After running away from his second job as an apprentice to an engraver, he spent some years wandering, penniless and doing odd jobs, before he was accepted into the household of Madame de Warens to whom he was pupil, factotum and lover. Having had no schooling himself, little experience of teaching and no children, he might seem a strange man to have written such influential books on education. *Emile*, Rousseau's most famous work on education, has had a lasting influence, bringing about something like a revolution in education. 'Reverse the usual practice', he wrote, 'and you will almost always do it right.'

I suspect that the phrase that occurs to many people in connection with Rousseau is 'the Noble Savage' but he was not advocating a return to the simple life away from civilization. He recognized that children ultimately have to take their place in society and should be prepared for this. However, he saw the home as the best place for social training. He felt that children needed to be kept from society until they had a firm base which would enable them to withstand the hazards of life. He did not believe in letting nature take its course, in allowing children to develop left to themselves. He thought that education was necessary but saw it more as a matter of guidance than instruction. 'Surround him with all the lessons you would have him learn without awaking his suspicions.' The child should learn through activities and experiences rather than books. Although he gave himself the role of tutor to his imaginary Emile, he made it clear that the best man to educate a boy is the boy's own father, just as a mother should educate a daughter. The parent has the role of guide and companion. 'The art of teaching,' he wrote, 'consists in making the pupil wish to learn.'

He maintained that it was important to be aware of the needs and abilities of the child rather than the demands of a curriculum or the expectations of adults: 'Childhood has its own ways of seeing, thinking, feeling', 'Every stage . . . has a perfection of its own'. He warned against forcing too early or robbing children of the joys of childhood. He believed that 'childhood is the sleep of reason' and that to deprive children of that sleep was as wrong as depriving them of real sleep – both were necessary for health. He saw the first twelve years of life as a time of preparation for education. His aim was 'a well-regulated liberty' but he noted that there was a difference between liberty and licence. He made the distinction between spoilt children and happy, self-reliant children.

So much of what Rousseau advocated has found its way into modern child-rearing practices, having been absorbed by educators such as Pestalozzi, Froebel and Montessori. Alas, his views on the education of girls are those of his time – based on ideas such as the importance of chastity, maintaining a 'good reputation' and the necessity for restraint and submissiveness. 'A woman's education must therefore be planned in relation to man. To be pleasing in his sight, to win his respect and love, to train him in childhood, to tend him in manhood, to counsel and console, to make his life pleasant and happy, these are the duties of woman for all time, and this is what she should be taught while she is young' (*Emile*). Poor girls. Yet this man who asked rhetorically, 'Does this mean that she must be brought up in ignorance and kept to housework only?' and maintained that 'A woman's honour does not depend on her conduct alone, but on her reputation . . . what people think of her matters as much as what she really is' had a long-term relationship with an uneducated and hard-working woman, an illiterate, who lived with him as a housekeeper. In his *Confessions*, he declared that he had all five of the children born to her packed off to the foundlings hospital straight after birth, a story which has understandably earned him a bad name. However no children have ever been traced and some researchers believe that, in fact, he had none – that this was a fabrication to hide the true reason for his childless state, whatever that was.

William Cobbett

William Cobbett's father taught him how to read, write and do elementary mathematics. He and his brothers learned a great deal about gardening and farming, both from listening to their parents and from years of practical experience helping on the family farm. When he was six he made himself a small garden on the top of a steep rock, carrying up the soil in his smock. At the age of eleven he ran away to Kew Gardens where he worked for a time.

As an adult, during a varied career, in which he twice went to America, had serious money problems, was prosecuted and imprisoned, Cobbett wrote a number of books and innumerable pamphlets on a wide range of subjects. He was a resolute moralist, tirelessly preaching the simple life and the virtues of self-sufficiency.

He educated his own children, seven of them, disapproving of schools 'over which parents have no control, and where nothing is taught but the rudiments of servility, pauperism and slavery' (*Cottage Economy*). He brought up his children in the country because he thought it was the best place for them. He worked from home, believing that they needed their father near them throughout the day:

> Many a score of paper I have written amidst the noise of children, and in my whole life I never bade them be still. When they grew up to be big enough to gallop about the house, I have, in wet weather, when they could not go out, written the whole day amidst noise that would have made some authors half mad. . . . That which you are pleased with, however noisy, does not disturb you (*Advice To Young Men*).

He maintained that he adhered rigidly to the principle that his children should never be in the care of anyone but himself or his wife, even temporarily, until they were old enough to look after themselves. If his friends invited him to visit but did not want his children's company, then they did not get his company either.

In the essay on home education, *To A Father* in *Advice to Young Men*, Cobbett wrote that a father's major concern should be the happiness of his offspring. He agreed with Rousseau that parents who thought that hardship and restraint was a good preparation for the future were likely to regret that they had not allowed childhood to be the time of joy that it should be. He claimed:

> I was resolved never to bring upon myself remorse from such a cause . . . to forego all means of making money . . . to give up every thing, to become a common labourer, rather than make my children lead a life of restraint and rebuke.

He put great emphasis on play and being out of doors. He disapproved of reading merely for pleasure – 'perhaps there are none more lazy, or more truly ignorant, than your everlasting readers. A book is an admirable excuse for sitting still. . . . In short, a young man should bestow his time upon no book, the contents of which he cannot apply to some useful purpose'. He thought that, where book-learning was incompatible with a child's happiness, it should be dispensed with. However he, himself, did enjoy reading – doubtless only 'useful' books! – and recognized their value as a source of information. Here is his description of life in the Cobbett household on wet days and in the evenings:

> A large strong table in the middle of the room, their mother sitting at her work, used to be surrounded by them, the baby, if big enough, set up in a high chair. Here were inks, pens, pencils, India-rubber and paper, all in abundance, and everyone scrambled about as he or she pleased. There were prints of animals of all sorts, books treating of them; others treating of gardening, of flowers, of husbandry, of hunting, shooting, fishing, coursing, planting, and in short, of everything with regard to which we had something to do. One would be trying to imitate my writing, another drawing pictures of some of our dogs or horses, a third poking over Bewick's Quadrupeds, and picking out what he had to say about them; but our book of never-failing resource was the French Maison Rustique. . . . Here were all the four-legged animals from the horse down to the mouse, portraits and all; all the birds, reptiles and insects . . . and there was I, in my leisure moments, to join this inquisitive group, to read the French and tell them what it meaned in English, when the picture did not sufficiently explain itself. (*Advice to Young Men*)

He asked, 'What need had we of schools? What need of teachers? What need of scolding and force to teach the children to read, write and love books?' He emphasised parental example; his patience with his children and his tirelessness and activity was the basis of their education. 'The book-learning crept in by imperceptible degrees. Children naturally want to be like their parents . . . and as I was always writing or reading, mine naturally desired to do something in the same way'.

In *Rural Rides*, he described how he taught his son arithmetic on a ride to Reigate when the boy was eleven years old. He introduced him to mental addition as they left home before day-break and progressed through the four rules first in whole numbers then in money, with sums written on paper when they stopped on the way.

By nightfall the boy could manage multiplication of pounds, shillings and pence. Cobbett commented on the ease of his method:

> I never yet saw in my house a child that was afraid; that was ever for a moment under any sort of apprehension, on account of the learning of anything; and I never in my life gave a command, an order, a request or even advice, to look into any book; and I am quite satisfied that the way to make children dunces, to make them detest books, and justify the detestation, is to tease them and bother them upon the subject.

Even the outspoken Cobbett was not free from 'meddling' friends and people who would ask why the children were not at school, saying things like, 'Bless me, so tall, and not learned any thing yet!' (*Advice To Young Men*.) His response was to reel off his children's practical accomplishments. He commented, 'How glad the children used to be, when they got clear of such criticising people! And how grateful they felt to me for the protection which they saw that I gave them against that state of restraint, of which other people's boys complained!' More disturbing to him were his own wife's anxieties on the subject – which she expressed 'perhaps twenty times a day' – but his resolve was unshaken; his children did not go to school.

Cobbett has received some scathing criticism over the years – the 1930s preface to *Advice to Young Men* calls him 'absurd', the 'sublime prig'. But, for me, his account of his correspondence with his children when he was imprisoned in Newgate for two years, following a libel case, redeems him totally and suggests that he really was the dedicated and loving father he says he was. His description of the gifts his children sent him give an insight into the warmth of a close and sensitive family. This is not the behaviour of unhappy children with an overbearing father. Every week a hamper was sent back and forth between the farm in Botley, Hampshire and the prison. This was, as he describes, 'our school'. Not only did it bring him fruit and other produce from the farm but also an account of all that was happening back at home:

> The journal used, when my son was the writer, to be interspersed with drawings of our dogs, colts, or any thing that he wanted me to have a correct idea of. The hamper brought me plants, bulbs and the like, that I might see the size of them; and always every one sent his or her most beautiful flowers; the earliest violets, and primroses, and cowslips and blue-bells; the earliest twigs of trees; and, in short, every thing that they thought calculated to delight me. The moment the hamper arrived, I, casting aside every thing else, set to work to answer every question, to give new directions, and to add anything

likely to give pleasure at Botley. Every hamper brought one 'letter', as they called it, if not more, from every child; and to every letter I wrote an answer, sealed up and sent to the party, being sure that that was the way to produce other and better letters . . . though they could not read what I wrote, and though their own consisted at first of mere scratches. . . .

His children took turns staying near him in hired rooms so that one of the abler writers could help manage his affairs while the others, young as they were, helped their mother run the farm.

He had some typical Cobbett advice for any parents who said they did not have enough time to educate their own children. He suggested that if they were to count up all the minutes in a day spent drinking coffee, lingering over meals, sitting up late, lying in bed 'while the sun and dew shine and sparkle for them in vain' and add to this all the time spent reading the 'useless' parts of the newspaper and books for mere 'personal amusement', then, seeing the total number of hours wasted, they would call their children home from school directly!

Women Writers

I have often been struck by the number of women writers who were educated at home. I know this is hardly surprising – even when sons were sent off to school, daughters were kept at home under the parental roof – and, as the employment of women outside the home was unthinkable among the better-off classes, a proportion of these home educated girls would inevitably turn to writing.

Just looking at the children's books on my daughters' shelves I see the names of several home educated women writers – Anna Sewell (*Black Beauty*), Ursula Moray Williams, (*The Adventures of the Little Wooden Horse*), Frances Hodgson Burnett (*The Secret Garden*), Eleanor Farjeon (poetry), Beatrix Potter (*The Tale of Peter Rabbit*) and Louisa May Alcott (*Little Women*) are a few that spring to mind.

The lives of the children's writers, Beatrix Potter and Louisa May Alcott, provide us with an interesting contrast. Beatrix Potter had a stifling childhood, mostly alone in the nursery of a house with few concessions to childhood. Her parents lived a rigidly disciplined and seemingly empty life, from which the child Beatrix was largely excluded. Her only brother was at boarding school. Family holidays provided an annual release from isolation, giving her access to a rural world which she came to love. She had some formal lessons with a governess, but interestingly she developed and grew in spite of the fact that she appeared to lack virtually all the ingredients of a happy childhood. And she wrote that hers was a happy childhood. Her own interests and activities contributed more to her education than the lessons. Deprived of stimulation and of daily contact with other children, she neverless found plenty to absorb her. She made collections of plants, animals and insects, smuggling home a wide variety of dead and live specimens. The live creatures were clandestinely cared for – a rabbit and a hedghog shared the nursery with her, snails were reared in a plant pot, mice concealed in a box and even bats lived in the parrot cage, swooping home to roost after their evening flight. Day to day records were kept of the animals' lives. The dead specimens were skinned, the bones boiled and the skeletons articulated and studied. Everything was drawn and painted; little books were sewn together; ink was mixed out of soot; a journal was kept in a private code – all in secret. It is easy to see the development of her little books for children from such a beginning.

In adulthood, she retained her childhood interest in nature, her careful observation and her self-motivated industry. She worked ⚊ long hours at the museums where she would go to draw. She studied geology, drawing and photographing fossils. She had a collection of drawings of fungi, hundreds of minutely detailed illustrations which she hoped would be used for a book. Her desire for recognition for her serious work came to nothing and she instead achieved fame for the stories and sketches she did for the amusement of her young relatives. She wrote of her childhood, 'Thank goodness, my education was neglected. . . . I am glad I did not go to school – it would have rubbed off some of the originality.'

Louisa May Alcott, the author of the American children's classic, *Little Women*, had an entirely different sort of childhood at home, free and full of affection. Her father wrote of his daughters in his diary, 'They are unwilling to pass their time within doors, or fix their thoughts on formal lessons. I spend an hour or more in the morning with them, but to small profit.' Louisa began to write a diary at the age of ten. She did not go to parties or the theatre but enjoyed village life, climbing trees, running races and leaping fences. As her father wrote, 'Their thoughts are on the distant hill, the wending river, the orchard, meadow or grove; and so I let them have the benefit of these.' Indoors she played with her sisters, with dolls. They acted out plays as well and helped with the housework. Her day began, as she described, rising at 5 a.m., having a bath (she declared she loved cold water – what enthusiasm for life, she must have been happy!) A singing lesson followed, then breakfast after which she washed dishes and played outside on the hill. Then there were lessons: spelling, arithmetic, reading stories and discussion. She would then read, play or go walking. She was devoted to her parents and sisters and her book was based on her experience of family life.

Virginia Woolf

When I discovered that Virginia Woolf was educated at home by her parents, I must confess my heart sank. As is well known, she had recurring periods of madness – I use the word both she and her biographers use – from adolescence on. She declared that she, as a girl, had been denied the educational opportunities given to her brothers. She portrayed her father as an overbearing tyrant. She ended her life in suicide. A worse advertisement for home education could hardly be imagined, yet I cannot pass her by: she was home-educated.

Looking more closely at her early life, quite a different picture emerges. I was surprised to discover she had a happy childhood; her father, however tyrannical he became when she was older, was remarkably affectionate towards her when she was a child – he was her favourite parent; she said later there was no one more lovable than he; from her earliest years she was encouraged to be a writer. Very real trauma precipitated her first breakdown: there was a family history of mental illness – her cousin died insane and her half-sister was put in an institution because of a 'mental deficiency' which was apparent soon after her birth. Knowing this, perhaps we can look at the education she received and see it as it was, the ideal training for a writer, rather than the reason for her madness, which it was not.

In her later writing she maintained that for a young woman of her generation to take up art or a profession, she had to make a break for freedom, away from the family and the prevailing ideals of womanhood. In her own case, a literary career –far from being a privilege denied to her or a freedom she had to struggle for – was accepted by her family from her earliest years. She grew up surrounded by people who placed great value on intellectual gifts. Her father was a well-known writer. Writers frequented the house. She and her sister agreed between themselves in childhood which one was going to be the writer and which the artist: her sister indeed became an artist, Vanessa Bell. At the age of five, Virginia would tell her father a story of her own making every night. He wrote of her when she was eleven, 'She takes in a great deal and really will be an author in time.' She was a much-praised child whose parents delighted in her intelligence and abilities. Each night when the children were in bed there would be a communal serial. Virginia, the second to youngest child, soon became the family story-teller.

Most of the teaching was done by the parents themselves. Before Virginia was seven, her mother taught her Latin, history and French, while the father taught mathematics, evidently not too successfully: Virginia counted on her fingers throughout her life. He had a hasty temper at times but could also be a patient and kindly father. When he was not trying to be a teacher, he delighted his children with his drawings and his exciting stories. He would read to the children each evening, prose during the week and poetry on Sundays. Virginia chiefly remembered the *Waverley* novels of Sir Walter Scott (in thirty-two volumes), Jane Austen and Nathaniel Hawthorne. At the end of each book, he would ask the children for their opinion of its merits. He clearly enjoyed their company and conversation.

'She always said that she had no education and I am inclined to agree with her if by education is meant learning things out of books,' said Vanessa of her sister. But, in spite of what they said, it seems they were far from uneducated and they must have learned a great deal from their reading. All through their childhood and adolescence, the sisters spent a considerable amount of time immersed in books. As Virginia grew older her father would guide her, lending her volumes from his library. He and she would take walks through Kensington Gardens every morning, their discussions about literature interspersed with thoughtful silences. She had an excellent writer's apprenticeship.

The sisters had two brothers near to them in age, as well as four older half-brothers and sisters from their parents' previous marriages. Her brothers received their elementary education at home, but were then sent off to school. Theirs was not wholly a leisured class; the boys were trained for their professional careers. When her older brother returned from his first school and told her what he had learned about the Greeks, Virginia resolved to learn Greek herself – which she did, at home. She felt that it was part of the world of privileges from which she, as a girl, was excluded. (It is part of a world of privileges from which most of mankind has been excluded.) She was expected to acquire female accomplishments. The sisters were taught drawing, dancing, singing, riding and 'graceful deportment'. They seemed not to have taken their classes very seriously, except drawing, which was a success, and piano which was considered a torment second only to going to the dentist.

However, away from their lessons, they happily set about educating themselves. Vanessa set herself the drawing exercises as outlined by Ruskin. For four years from the age of nine, Virginia produced a weekly newspaper, aimed at an adult readership and wittily written, to judge from extracts. Before she was 13 she was trying to imitate the novels of Hawthorne in her writing.

During their childhood they spent the summers at their rented house in Cornwall. It had an acre or two of gardens – terraces divided by escallonia hedges, with a fountain and all kinds of summer fruits, shrubberies, lawns and private places – leading down to the sea. They would accompany their father on long walks, during which they would be encouraged to study botany, though their more enduring interest was the collection of moths and butterflies. The house was the setting for her novel *To the Lighthouse*. Mrs Ramsay of the novel was based on Virginia's mother, a tireless visitor of the sick, regarded by some as a saintly woman. Mr Ramsay was based on her father but the love and affection he showed her during her childhood seems to have been left out. The summer idylls in Cornwall came to an end when Virginia was 13. They had been, as her biographer Quentin Bell writes, 'the happiest time of a happy childhood' but all that soon changed.

Their mother died. The house at St Ives was given up. The bereavement itself was terrible enough for the adolescent Virginia, but the circumstances following added horror to grief. In his mourning, her father retreated into his own feelings, becoming more like the tyrant portrayed. At times he would descend into histrionics, self-pitying and wallowing in his misery. The sisters began to see him as feeding off the strength of the women around him, dependent but dominating. Stella, the girls' older half-sister, took over the running of the household but she too died soon after. This confirmed their view of their father as a tyrannical destroyer of women. Their older half-brother helped them to extend this view to men generally. He, a grown man, source of many outings and treats, model of Victorian respectability – and hypocrisy – had molested Virginia when she was younger. Now, masquerading as their protector and comforter, he had freer access to force his sexual attentions upon her. The mental illness that was to dog her throughout her life now set in.

Of course, some commentators point to Virginia Woolf's education at home as a contributing factor to her breakdown. I hold the view that extreme intelligence and intense intellectual activity is not the cause of mental illness but rather, in certain individuals, accompanied by it. (Less a case of 'You mustn't over-tax your brain!' – as my Great Aunt Hilda would say – and more that genius is sometimes allied to madness.) I have read that people who go to school have more chance, statistically, of going into a mental hospital at some time in their life than they have of going to university. Well, it's an interesting thought, something to bear in mind when considering the possibility of mental instability in the home-educated.

Jane Austen

Like Virginia Woolf, Jane Austen declared herself to be under-educated: 'I think I can boast myself with all possible vanity the most

unlearned and uninformed being that ever dared to be an authoress.'
There the comparisons could end. Jane Austen has been described as
one of the few people of genius who got through to adulthood
without periods of feeling depressed, lonely, misunderstood or
rebellious. She was fortunate in being born into a happy, affectionate
family, with loving, cheerful parents. There were no tragedies or
trauma. Family life was good-tempered and well-mannered, with
none of the purple rages or 'beserker fits' that Virginia Woolf and her
father were disposed to by temperament. Jane Austen lived a life that
seems to have been happy and contented.

She was especially close to her sister, Cassandra, who was two
years her senior. When Jane was seven they were both sent to be
educated by a woman distantly related to the family, an arrangement
that came to an end within a few months. The brief experiment was
not a success: the woman was stiff and formal and it seems,
irresponsible – the girls fell seriously ill and Jane came close to dying.
The episode is described as a shadow falling over a hitherto sunny
existence. A year later another school was tried. Her parents thought
she was too young to go but as her mother said, 'If Cassandra was
going to have her head cut off, Jane would insist on sharing her fate'!
After a year their parents, perhaps realizing that the education they
were receiving was not of a very good quality, brought them home
again to join their brothers. It is interesting that in the Austen
household, where the education of boys was – as elsewhere – held to
be of paramount importance, it was the boys who were educated
wholly at home. Her brothers were taught by their father until they
left home for university or to join the navy.

There was not a great deal of formal teaching at home for the
sisters, who largely educated themselves. They embroidered,
sketched, played the piano – there were probably instructors for
some subjects – they shared in the lively and intelligent conversations
that characterized their household, helped in the house, went
walking and, long before their teens, spent most of their day writing
and reading. Her father, a clergyman of the wealthier sort, had a
great love of literature and regularly read aloud to his family. Her
mother was well-known for her witty impromptu stories. Amateur
theatricals were a great favourite with the family: they clearly
enjoyed life together. It was 'a life made pleasant by the flow of
native wit with all the fun and nonsense of a large and clever family'.
In spite of her claim to be the most unlearned and uninformed being,
she was well-read in prose and poetry, had a knowledge of history
and French as well as some Italian. By the time she was in her teens,
she had already read widely enough to have discovered most of the
books that were to remain her favourites throughout her lifetime.

She was well acquainted with many works of literature, particularly those of the great 18th century writers. She had the run of her father's library and was free to read such works as *Tristam Shandy* and *Tom Jones* which, in a later age, might have been considered unsuitable for a young girl. As her biographer David Cecil writes, 'She had a very good kind of education, that which comes from living with clever people'. The world she lived in was secure, peaceful and stable. She had the time and freedom from pressure to follow her interests and to develop her talent unforced.

The Brontes: Charlotte, Emily and Anne

Perhaps it is the Brontes who provide the best-known example of home education. We have probably all heard the story of their isolated childhood, overshadowed by tragedy, of the fantasy kingdoms they created together and the extraordinary collection of miniature home-made books that they wrote about their imaginary worlds. We can picture them growing up in the parsonage surrounded by the bleakness of the moors and overlooking the graveyard of Haworth church, of which their father was clergyman.

Unlike the more comfortably-off women of their day, once they reached adulthood they had to work outside the home to earn a living, as teachers and governesses. Their writing was not the by-product of enforced leisure.

They went to school for only very brief periods in their lives – Branwell, their brother, not at all – and so were educated at home by their father, and to a great extent by themselves. The eldest child, Maria, patiently taught the younger children how to read. They were very shy, kept apart as they were from the local children. Their father was solitary by nature and did not encourage them to mix.

There were six children born within seven years. Shortly after Anne's birth, their mother died and an aunt took on the running of the household. The two eldest girls, Maria and Elizabeth, were sent to school when they were aged eleven and nine. Charlotte and Emily followed a little later. It was partly a charity school, with low fees, like the institution described in *Jane Eyre*. The discipline was rigorous, the teaching harsh, the food inadequate and badly cooked. Maria, the model for Helen Burns in *Jane Eyre*, was persecuted by a teacher who disliked her 'cast of character'. She developed tuberculosis and died within a year of going to school. A few weeks later, Elizabeth was sent home with a fever and died soon after. Charlotte and Emily were quickly taken back home, to their intense relief. During her ten months at the school, Charlotte was well-behaved and hard-working but inwardly she raged, blaming the school for the sufferings of her sisters. The experience left a mark on her which lasted all her life.

After attending her first school, the entry in the school register described Charlotte thus, 'Reads tolerably. Writes indifferently. Ciphers a little, and works neatly. Knows nothing of grammar, geography, history or accomplishments. Altogether clever of her age, but knows nothing systematically'. Although the school remarked on the weaknesses of the education they had received at home, Mr Bronte noted the signs of his children's gifts which, he wrote in a letter to Mrs Gaskell, he had 'seldom or never before seen in any of their age'. The school's estimation of their talents certainly did not tally with other reports.

The children had virtually no toys – their father did not believe in indulgences – and few friends outside their own family. However they were not unhappy. 'We wove a web in childhood', wrote Charlotte. From an early age, they wrote plays in which the heroes were Wellington, Napoleon, Hannibal and Caesar. They invented kingdoms and immersed themselves in a world of make-believe adventure. A set of wooden soldiers inspired a complex saga. It was Branwell, their brother, who conceived of producing a periodical for the soldiers, small enough to fit into a toy soldier's hand and written in a microscopic script, designed to resemble print. Charlotte, now the eldest of the four, managed to take over the editorship of the periodical. She and Branwell wrote the chronicles of Glasstown and Angria, while Emily and Anne were responsible for the literature of Gondal, another kingdom. The secret manuscripts were more extensive than their published works.

Their days together were to be disrupted once more. Mr Bronte fell seriously ill and, although he recovered, the incident made him concerned about his offspring's ability to earn their living. Charlotte was sent off to another school, Roe Head, at the age of 14 for a year and a half. Although her studies at home had been irregular, she soon rose to first place in the class and was described by her friends as being at the head of the whole school in terms of intellectual ability. Emily also had a period at Roe Head during her teens but only stayed three months. Her place was then taken up by Anne the youngest. From the age of 16 Charlotte helped to educate her younger sisters, spending her spare time reading and writing.

Perhaps it seems surprising that a mystic and poet, the author of *Wuthering Heights* – Emily – was the one to take on the cooking and most of the household work. She was the sister least able to cope with life away from home. Mrs Gaskell's description of her stay at Roe Head shows us something of the reason for this:

Liberty was the breath of Emily's nostrils, without it she

perished. The change from her own home to a school, and from her own very noiseless, very secluded, but unrestricted and inartificial mode of life, to one of disciplined routine . . . was what she failed in enduring. Her nature proved too strong for her fortitude. . . . In this struggle her health was quickly broken. . . .

The kitchen door of the parsonage opened straight out onto fields which stretched to the moors. Emily, usually so shy and withdrawn in company, showed absolute self-assurance and delight at life when on the moor: her spirit was as if liberated. 'Every moss, every flower, every tint and form, were noted and enjoyed. Emily especially had a gleesome delight in these nooks of beauty. . . .' wrote Ellen Nussey in *Reminiscences of Charlotte Bronte*. In the Gondal writings, by Emily and Anne, the recurrent theme is the expanse and freedom of the moors contrasted with imprisonment and despair. These images occur more frequently as the sisters are forced to spend time away from home.

Conclusion

I could not help noticing that many eminent people did not have what we would call a broad education. I noticed this first among the artists and musicians. Our modern idea seems to be that a broad curriculum offers all children the scope to develop their talents. In contrast to this, many great artists of the past received a training in art, often apprenticed at a young age so that they learned by working in a studio. I cannot help but wonder what would have happened to Rembrandt (or Raphael, Leonardo, Rubens, Durer . . . the list can be as long as you like) in our modern school system. They were educated in their own homes and then apprenticed at the age of twelve or thirteen. Much the same could be said of composers. Bach, Beethoven, Mendelssohn, Mozart, Vivaldi, Weber were directed towards music by their parents in their earliest years – what we would today consider a lop-sided education. Could we argue that they were lacking as a result of it?

Although in some cases the picture looks as if it might have been bleak – I do not envy some of them their lives – it did make me think that nowadays we are over-anxious, as if we think there is only one right way to bring up children: nothing but eleven years of compulsory schooling will do; nothing but a standard education is right. Reading modern books on child-rearing, it does sometimes seem that if you put a foot wrong on the path, you'll crush the bud before it gets the chance to flower. Perhaps the very people, such as A.S. Neill, Maria Montessori and Rudolf Steiner, who have given us such valuable insight into childhood, have in fact added to this anxiety. In showing us a new and better way to bring up our children, they also show us the mistakes we make and the damage we may do when we don't adhere to their methods.

Surely I am not the only parent who has read Leboyer after the event, or *Kindergarten Is Too Late* when it *was* too late, and felt guilt or regret? Retrospective guilt must be a particular feature of our times, made possible thanks to our understanding of psychology. (Christina Hardyment's study of babycare literature over the past two hundred years, *Dream Babies*, links the beginnings of psychology with the rise of the 'neurotic baby syndrome'.) Nowadays we are assured from all sides not only that we damage our children by our actions, but also that we unwittingly did so from the moment they were born. Or as A.S. Neill wrote, 'Unfreedom begins with birth. Nay, it begins long before birth. If a repressed woman with a rigid body bears a child, who can say what effect the maternal rigidity has on the newborn baby?' Help! What hope is there for any of us? Is it any wonder that many parents today feel so unsure in their role, as if – whatever they do – they are doing it all wrong?

Yet people like Neill brought rays of sunshine and sanity into our understanding of our children. Perhaps we should realize that life does not stand still: the theories were an essential development in their time, but do not provide all the answers for ever. None of the theorists give us the complete and enduring picture, but small pieces of jigsaw we may be able to fit somewhere into our own framework.

The idea of psychological damage of children by misguided parents abounds in modern childcare literature. Steiner tells us that the small child is a sense organ which can be damaged by observing our wrongful actions. Montessori uses terms like 'deviated' of children who do not fit her criterion of the 'normal' – due to wrong upbringing. Neill writes about free children being happy and well-balanced, contrasting these with the sick and neurotic majority who as adults will endanger the world.

Sometimes Victor and I wonder whether our society's obsession with the 'well-adjusted personality' is right. Could it be that some of the apparently happy, well-balanced, healthy-minded people may also be a danger to the world – those who always want to look on the bright side and ignore the dangers and the very real horrors of life. It often seems to us that those who suffer when they consider the state of things may be the world's best hope of salvation. In holding up health and well-adjustedness as examples of an ideal, we should not write off everyone else. There has to be room for introverts, for the children who keep to the edges of the playground, for all those many people who do not fit the mould of the norm.

Appendix II

Education Otherwise

I would wholeheartedly recommend that anyone considering home education for their children, contact Education Otherwise. This is a self-help organization run by and for families who are interested in home-based education. Membership would be especially valuable during the early years when you are starting out on home education. As well as the advice and information that they are able to give you – drawing on many families' experiences over the past decade – Education Otherwise is a source of support, fellow-feeling, warmth and friendship: here are other families with aims and difficulties similar to your own.

Education Otherwise – or E.O. as it is familiarly known – was formed by a small number of parents at the beginning of 1977. Since then membership has grown steadily. It now stands at about 1800, individuals and families, spread throughout Britain, with a small number overseas. Membership is open to anyone, whether they are practising home education or not. Education Otherwise takes its name from the phrase in the Education Act which gives us the 'or otherwise' option. Its aim is to offer a service to its members and to establish the freedom of all families to make responsible choices about education.

The group's members have turned to home education – or support the principle of home education – for a variety of different reasons. For some, it is as a result of their own or their children's experiences – perhaps harmful experiences – at school. For others, it is because of their fundamental convictions about bringing up children. There is a healthy diversity of opinions and beliefs among its members, just as there is a wide range of lifestyles. E.O. does not therefore recommend any 'correct' method of education or provide teaching syllabuses and materials. No one view on education would be acceptable to all its members. It is an association of people with a common aim – to support the freedom of families to keep, rather than to delegate, responsibility for their children's education.

E.O. is a registered charity and a limited company. It does not have any source of funding other than members' subscriptions and donations. Its existence and running depends wholly on the work and commitment of members who volunteer to take on certain jobs. It has no paid officials and no offices. Decisions about policy are made at meetings to which all members are invited. At a local level, in each county there is a Co-ordinator who deals with enquiries and puts new members in contact with other families in their area. Any specific queries may be referred to someone with the appropriate specialist knowledge. In this way there is a local support and information network – very important when, for example, you are first encountering your Local Education Authority – backed up by the national network. The Co-ordinator will usually be a parent with experience of school-age children learning at home.

E.O. arranges national events several times a year – residential weekends, conferences and meetings. On a local level there may be joint outings, picnics, regular or irregular social meetings, workshops – whatever the members themselves decide to organize.

Membership is through an annual subscription fee. Low-income families who cannot afford the fee can pay a reduced rate or, in cases of exceptional hardship, the fee will be waived altogether.

New members are sent E.O.'s booklets dealing with aspects of education at home. Non-members may purchase these separately, direct from E.O.:

School Is Not Compulsory is an excellent guide to the legal considerations of not sending a child to school. It contains information about the law, as well as advice about the relationship you might expect with the L.E.A. and the procedure you are likely to have to go through, based on members' accounts of their own experiences.

Early Years is a useful source book about the education of younger children. A book for the teen years is in preparation.

Members are also sent an extensive Contact List which lists the names and addresses of E.O. families, along with the names and ages of their children. Their interests and skills may be indicated on the list, along with any resources and facilities they wish to offer other families. You can choose whether or not you want to have your details circulated in this way. The list enables members to contact each other, not only locally but also throughout the country, even overseas. Some offer holiday accommodation. Many members welcome visitors.

It is the Contact List, I feel, that is the very heart of E.O. It is this that provides a family – a family who might otherwise feel isolated in their school-orientated community – with the means of meeting like-minded families and exchanging ideas (or meeting unlike-minded families and discovering totally new ways of looking at life!) and of making firm new friends, adults as well as children. We have certainly met some of the nicest people we know – with some of the finest children – through Education Otherwise. As one member said, 'Many of our closest friends have been made through national meetings of E.O. I wonder how many people could say they could travel almost anywhere in the British Isles and be able to stay with friends.'

The Newsletter, issued six times a year, contains notices of meetings, articles, book reviews and letters, including personal accounts and ideas on learning at home. Families newly embarking on home education are likely to find the Newsletter particularly reinforcing. It was my introduction to E.O.: it was what made me realize that home education can work in less than ideal surroundings. Most of the accounts from other families that I quote in Chapter 9 are drawn from the Newsletter.

Many parents new to home education are concerned about the possibility of legal proceedings: it is reassuring to know that the majority of E.O.'s members have encountered no problems of this sort. Sometimes a family, already embroiled with the L.E.A., approaches E.O. for help. Given good advice, information and reassuring support, they may get through their difficulties and into calmer waters surprisingly quickly. We have ourselves witnessed families making the transition from a distressing crisis, from which they could see no way out, to a situation where they were able to resolve their problems with growing confidence. As well as giving sound legal advice, E.O. can also recommend, if necessary, solicitors or child psychologists who are sympathetic to the principle of children learning at home. There is a Legal Group to advise those who find themselves in conflict with their Local Authority as well as a Family Support Fund to help with legal fees.

There is a support group for parents of children with Special Educational Needs. The number of families who are choosing home education for their 'special' children is growing and this provides a pool of information and support.

One family has started up an Information Resource Centre (see page 182 for fuller details). There has been a proposal recently that E.O. could raise money to provide regional resource centres with books and equipment – including the expensive science equipment needed for practical experiments – to which members could have access through a borrowing scheme. It sounds like a superb idea, which I look forward to hearing more about. As the number of families involved in home learning grows – and the trend has been consistently upwards over the past ten years – there should be more opportunities for this sort of project.

Contact Education Otherwise through your local Co-ordinator (her address may be obtained from the Citizens' Advice Bureau or the register of local clubs and societies at the public library) or through their central address.

Appendix III

Resources

ADVISORY CENTRE FOR EDUCATION (A.C.E.)

The Advisory Centre for Education provides a service for parents with questions or problems relating to education in state-maintained schools. This advice service, and any follow-up help that is needed, is provided free of charge. A.C.E. is a registered charity, working independently of Government departments. A quarter of the queries they receive are about Special education referral, assessment and allocation procedures. They also receive queries concerning school allocation, discipline, etc. They do not give comparative information about individual schools or L.E.A.s, nor do they provide information about schools in the private sector.

A.C.E. produces a range of publications, obtainable by post, dealing with educational matters and parents' and children's rights. Your local reference library will probably have copies of some A.C.E. publications including the A.C.E. *Bulletin*. The *Bulletin*, 6 issues a year, gives up-to-date information on D.E.S. and H.M.I. Reports as well as newly published educational books, journals and reports from various organizations.

Other publications include the *Special Education Handbook* and *Education A–Z – Where to Look Things Up*. They also supply information sheets covering various educational matters.

DISTANCE LEARNING

The only British-based correspondence courses I know of specifically for the general education of the under-14s are available through the World-wide Education Service (see page 191).

See under Montessori (page 186) for courses for parents on child rearing and Montessori education.

G.C.S.E.s AND G.C.E.s

There are several correspondence colleges offering examination courses and introductory courses for people wishing to study at home. Perhaps the best known are Wolsey Hall and the National Extension College. Although their courses are geared to adult home-learners, they accept younger students. Wolsey Hall advise that, in their experience, school-age students following examination courses at home need full parental supervision and help as well as the service provided.

The National Extension College is a non-profit-making organization which, as well as offering correspondence courses, runs courses in collaboration with local colleges (see Flexistudy below). Their Learning Support Department gives advice on courses.

Flexistudy

Some local colleges run Flexistudy courses, combining correspondence course materials from the N.E.C. with tutorials at the college and access to college facilities – including laboratories, where appropriate. Flexistudy was designed to fill the gap between home learning and regular college attendance. The student is appointed a tutor who gives guidance throughout the course. Tutorials may be in groups or by individual appointment (included in the cost). Arrangements vary from centre to centre, so contact your local college for details. For a list of participating colleges contact the N.E.C.

There may be a lower age limit: my local college stipulates a minimum of four years' secondary schooling (or equivalent) before enrolment.

EDUCATIONAL SUPPLIES

You can buy the same materials and equipment that schools use, from educational suppliers, by mail order – just as teachers do. The two major suppliers are Hestair Hope and E.J. Arnold. Their full catalogues are large (about the size of a telephone directory), beautifully produced and show a very impressive range of equipment for use from pre-school to secondary level.

However, the problem, sometimes, is getting hold of a catalogue. These are obviously very expensive to produce and are intended for big spenders like schools. When asking for a catalogue, tell them your children are educated at home and, if you know other interested families, you could ask for a catalogue to share.

V.A.T. is payable in addition. Hestair Hope do not charge for delivery. Some of the more standard toys are usually cheaper in the shops, but the specialist equipment – for mathematics, science, art and craft – is hard to track down in order to make comparisons. We have found the catalogues substantially cheaper in several instances. (A Tasco Pocket microscope, for example, was a couple of pounds cheaper from Hestair Hope than from the stockist in town.) The drawback on some stationery items is that they have to be bought in bulk, although white card and craft paper can be bought in quite small quantities much cheaper than at a stationers.

E.J. Arnold, under the name Arnold-Wheaton at the same address, also have educational book catalogues. Specify the age-group and the subjects you are interested in.

If you can shop in person at Hestair Hope's Oldham premises you get a 20% discount.

The toy manufacturers, Galt, have an educational supplies catalogue which, in my experience, they are reluctant to send out. If you can get a catalogue, though, they do allow a discount to Education Otherwise members – and others, perhaps – although they charge for delivery.

If you cannot get a Galt schools' supplies catalogue but have a Galt toy stockist near you it may be an idea to ask if you can look at their catalogue. They may be willing to order for you – my local toy shop does.

Playgroup 'Bulk Buys' Another possible source of equipment, paints, paper, plastic aprons and more, is the Pre-school Playgroup Association. They buy equipment in bulk and are able to resell to playgroup leaders at special 'bulk buy' sessions. The prices are consequently very low. In some areas they let parents come to these sessions, too. In several large towns there are also general 'toy bulk buys', well worth a visit. The Information Officer at the P.P.A.'s London address says there is currently no central register of these 'bulk buy' sessions and, unfortunately, no national policy on opening the doors to home-educating parents, so it very much depends on the local branches. Make enquiries locally.

Discounts When I was buying an instrument at a music shop recently, the assistant conversationally asked me which school my children went to. On hearing that they learn at home, he promptly informed me that I – as a teacher! – was entitled to a teacher's discount of 10%. Perhaps there are other shops who will offer similar discounts on educational supplies. (My mind first sprang to bookshops but there is retail price maintenance on books which does not allow shops to sell below the cover price under normal circumstances.)

HOME-MADE EQUIPMENT

With a supply of white card you can make your own educational games and cards, particularly useful for younger children, easily and without great expense. Your own equipment can be pitched at the right level for your child and be tailored around her particular interests or abilities.

Don't feel that your home-made equipment will be inferior to that used in schools. Teachers make their own teaching aids, too. You can almost certainly do better than you imagine. It is worth looking at educational games in the shops or, if you have one, in a schools' supplies catalogue for ideas.

White card   White card can be bought from Hestair Hope in packs of ten large sheets (635 x 508 mm or 25 x 20 ins) for less than a third of the price charged in the shops. It is available in whole sheets or ready-cut into smaller sizes. There is a variety of thicknesses. I found the 6-sheet thickness fine for general purposes like card games. The 3-sheet thickness is all right for children to cut and fold to make model buildings, geometical 'solids' or Christmas cards, but too thin for games where it will need to withstand handling. If you want to use flashcards and don't feel like cutting up all that cardboard, blank index cards (from a stationer's shop) will work out cheaper than postcards.

Plastic Adhesive Film   Plastic adhesive film, sold by the roll, cheapest in large stationer's shops, will lengthen the lives of your home-made games and stop them getting smudged. It is good, too, for giving a new lease of life to even the flimsiest picture paperback.

Rubber Stamps   In the educational supplies catalogues there are many different rubber stamps: for printing geometric shapes, coins, pictures showing fractions, animals, even developing frog spawn – none of which are really necessary. But if, like me, you soon tire of drawing round egg cups and filling in little clock faces you might be glad to buy a clock-face rubber stamp. Galt have a good clear one, with or without numerals, available in their schools' supplies range.

Tactile Letters   Sandpaper letters are standard Montessori equip-ment, recommended for essential tactile experience for younger children. I made our set using fine sandpaper stuck on white card. It is best to use a base line on which all letters sit, with plenty of room above and below, bearing in mind some letters have descenders. However, I must say that I found that the tips of my fingers quickly felt over-sensitive to the touch of sandpaper, even very fine sandpaper as recommended. I wondered if it would anaesthetize a small child's touch to use them. Although I made a set, the children were never very interested.

Felt I found much better. It can be stuck onto card and does not fray. I cannot see what is so desirable about sandpaper – virtually anything you make letters out of would provide a tactile experience and allow the 'multi-sensory' approach to learning. There is plenty of room for experiment and the more you involve the children themselves in the process of actually making the letters the faster they will learn them. The possibilities are endless: you can make all sorts of letter shapes, permanent or temporary – edible as well.

Writing Practice   To encourage correct letter formation, I found that writing in salt was popular. Use a dark coloured baking tray or dish, pour in the salt and show your child how to 'write' letters with an index finger. A shake rubs them out again. My children enjoyed doing this at three or four years. I found this more successful than trying to get them to trace round letter shapes which my independent daughters would always want to do in their own way, not the 'correct' way I showed them.

INFORMATION RESOURCE CENTRE

E.O. members Diane and Andy Anderson run an Information Resource Centre to help people find out about educational books and materials. They welcome letters or calls, by telephone or in person, from anyone who wants information. What they don't know, they will try to find out. In my own contact with them, I found them very helpful and I am sure their service could be extremely useful to many parents.

An order form is available so that enquirers can send for computer-printed information sheets listing recommended books and materials on a range of subjects as well as ideas for 'without a textbook' learning.

The service is free, but there is a very small charge for information sheets to cover printing costs. They receive no funding from any source, so please always send a stamped, self-addressed envelope when writing to them.

LIBRARY FACILITIES

Make enquiries about getting extra tickets; some libraries allow extra for teachers and students. You could say you, and your spouse if you have one, come into both categories. Ask also about extended periods of loan on books needed for study – some libraries allow this for teachers and students, sometimes for months at a stretch.

Ordering Books   You can order any books you cannot find on the shelves. There may be a small fee for this to cover postage, although in mobile libraries this may even be free. They will track books down for you, even those long out of print. Books not available in the county will be obtained from further afield through the inter-library loan system.

Record Libraries   Larger libraries often have a record section. Apart from music, they may very well have records or tapes of works of literature – very useful for 'O' or 'A' Level English. Shakespeare, or Chaucer, is a lot easier to understand if you listen to it while following the text.

They may also have foreign language courses – very expensive to buy – on record or tape. These come complete with their accompanying books so that you can learn French, German or whatever language takes your fancy, in the comfort of your own home, for a matter of pence.

Other Libraries   Apart from public libraries, lending and reference, there are other libraries to which you may be allowed access. Universities and colleges have very good libraries – open long hours – and although they may not let you take books away, they will often let you use the facilities for reference.

Libraries in colleges of further education or technical colleges are a good source of information about public examinations – G.C.S.E.s and G.C.E.s. They may have examination syllabuses and old papers that you can look at. They may also have prospectuses and other information about entrance to university and other higher education courses.

Teachers' Centres   If you are very fortunate you may live in an area where there is a Teacher's Centre or a special library for teachers. As a parent educating children at home, you may be able to use their facilities. One mother, Antonia Young, made an interesting discovery while trying to track down a particular reading scheme. She had ordered a couple of the reading books through a bookshop, but they took six weeks to arrive. As her daughter then read through them within two days, this made her realize how expensive and time-wasting this procedure was. Her local library could not help her as they had a policy of not stocking school reading books and they took a long time to obtain them from elsewhere. She made her discovery at a library in a nearby city:

> It was the Children's Librarian there who helpfully advised me, firstly, that as a home educator I am entitled to the special facilities open to teachers, and secondly, that from their Education Department on the 7th floor, teachers could obtain books which are not available to the general public. On reaching the 7th floor, my arrival was welcomed by a waiting librarian who took me straight to their shelf of Hummingbird books. She asked no documentation from me, not even a library card, but regretted that I could only take out 30 books at a time, and only for a term at a time (though these could be renewed by phone). It feels as though I've discovered a goldmine!

MATHEMATICS

The Cockcroft Report   Some parents will feel nervous about their
ability to teach – or help their children learn – mathematics. Perhaps
it will be some small comfort to them to hear that a fifth of all maths
teaching in secondary schools is in the hands of teachers with no
training in the subject. This estimation was reported by the
Cockcroft Committee in 1982 after their inquiry into mathematics
teaching in schools. (Your local reference library should have a copy
of the Report, published by H.M.S.O.)

The Committee called for major changes in the way maths is
taught. They rejected the call for a 'back to basics' approach which
would concentrate on the arithmetical skills of addition, subtraction,
multiplication and division. Instead they felt that what was needed
was an understanding of maths and an ability to recognize
mathematical situations in everyday life. Knowing how to
manipulate figures is of limited use when children do not understand
how to use their knowledge, or why they are following the
procedures they have been taught. Parents might bear this in mind
instead of feeling anxious about teaching their children what they
remember as 'classroom' maths.

Children – even those who are bright and are doing well at school
– often follow computational routines blindly without ever
understanding why. When they make mistakes, they are frequently
unable to recognize them because their understanding of what they
are doing is so limited. The child needs to be able to recognize there is
a connection between the sum on the page and what she knows about
the world. Discussion and practical work are an essential element in
helping your child to understand maths.

The Cockcroft Report makes some interesting recommendations.
In the primary years children should not be expected to move too
quickly to written recording. In the early stages oral and mental
work should be a major part of learning. The Committee identified a
wide range of attainment among children – a 'seven-year difference'
in the age at which children show understanding of certain topics. In
the secondary years the syllabus followed by most pupils has been
very strongly influenced by the content of the 'O' Level syllabuses –
which were only intended for the top 25%. The result of this, the
Committee found, was that very many pupils failed to develop a
confident approach and did not master those topics that were within
their capabilities. This meant that three quarters of the school
population were receiving an unsuitable mathematical education,
one that was hampering them rather than helping them. The
Committee called for the syllabus to be redesigned from 'the bottom

upwards'. Those who are optimistic will look to the G.C.S.E. examination syllabus to change all this. I suppose I am a pessimist.

The report outlines a foundation list of mathematical topics which the Committee recommends should form the basis of the secondary school syllabus, particularly for the less able 40% of pupils. It is worth looking at and might provide an interesting basic check-list for the teen years. Again, the emphasis is largely on the practical applications likely to be encountered in everyday adult life.

Mathematics Schemes   If you are still nervous about mathematics at home, you might want to use a structured scheme – the sort of scheme that schools follow. Rather than adhere to the books rigidly, you can use them as a back-up to the essential practical work and discussion of any other maths you might do. For the primary years with Hosanna we used the *Mathematics For Schools* series by Harold Fletcher (Addison Wesley) as a base from which we departed, returning periodically. There are several schemes currently available. Contact the Resources Information Centre for other titles (see page 182). Buying a whole scheme at once is obviously expensive, as well as being an act of faith. For the primary years, bookshops with educational sections or large branches of stationers like W.H. Smiths or John Menzies may stock individual workbooks.

We found that the major drawback of the scheme we used with Hosanna was that it tended to be too repetitive. There was far too much colouring in called for in the early stages followed by too many columns of sums as the books progressed. I can see that repetitive work is a useful way of keeping a class of thirty busy – they are designed for schools, after all. But if a child has grasped an idea, there is no point in labouring away for pages.

The strength of the series we used is in its *Teacher's Resource Books*. The one covering infant level mathematics (Mathematics For Schools, Teacher's Resource Book Level 1) is particularly good, containing lots of suggestions for activities and games to give background experience as well as frequent 'check-ups' so that you know what should have been grasped before you move onto the next section. Each page of the workbooks is reproduced in the *Teacher's Resource Book*. If you do not want your child to plough through the workbooks, you might prefer to go through the resource book, working and discussing with your child, without a great deal of written recording. I have preferred this approach with Fiorin. However, she has been such a keen workbook user (never having been actively encouraged to use them!) that, in the early stages, she has worked through the colourful *Now I Can . . .* series by Michael Holt (Belitha Press – Collins Educational). They give a lively introduction to written mathematics in very gentle stages.

Cuisenaire Rods A surprising amount of the mathematics we have done with our children has involved Cuisenaire rods at some stage. We have found them indispensible. They are visually pleasing as well as an interesting size for small fingers to manipulate – children love building and playing with them. Using them to work out mathematical problems, a child can understand much better than when she is wrestling with abstract figures and ideas. The rods are available direct from the Cuisenaire Company or from good toyshops.

MONTESSORI

My introduction to Montessori was through her book *The Secret of Childhood*, which sets out the ideas behind the method. She wrote a number of books outlining her theories and describing the materials but some of them, inevitably, now seem quaintly old-fashioned.

Montessori's didactic materials can be bought through the St Nicholas Training Centre or the London Montessori Centre: apply for price lists and details. Galt and Hestair Hope supply reasonably priced (non-wooden) Montessori geometric insets. There are two books written by Elizabeth Hainstock, one covering the pre-school years and the other the primary school years, for parents wishing to make their own materials for teaching in the home (see bibliography).

The premises of the Montessori Society are shared by a Montessori school and the Maria Montessori Training Organization which offers a full-time course leading to a diploma.

The London Montessori Centre offers full-time and correspond-ence courses for would-be Montessori teachers. They have a correspondence course for parents who are interested in the application of Montessori child rearing practices in the home.

The St Nicholas Training Centre for the Montessori Method of Education offers full and part-time courses. They also offer external diploma (correspondence) courses which were specifically devised to help parents who wish to teach their children at home, although they are also suitable for training teachers in the Method. I was interested to see that the courses extend to cover the education of children up to the age of twelve rather than only the nursery years. The Principal of the Centre expressed particular personal interest in home education when I contacted her for information.

MUSIC

Many music shops have a system where you can hire an instrument while you decide if you want to buy it. You pay a deposit, keep the instrument for an agreed period of time, paying a hire fee which is then deducted from the cost if you wish to keep it.

If you are buying an instrument for 'educational purposes' – for your home-educated child to learn – ask about a teacher's discount.

My local music shop has practice rooms for hire, at what seems to me a ludicrously low hourly rental. Such facilities also exist in other towns. If your child is unwilling to practise at home – or if you want to give your neighbours a quiet hour or two – she may be more inclined to practise if you go to a real music room complete with music stand and one (or even two!) pianos. You can take your own portable instruments, of course.

READING, SPELLING AND BOOKS

Learning to Read, and Spelling There are two major schools of thought on the teaching of reading. One favours the 'look-say' method where children learn by recognizing whole words; the other favours the phonic method where they learn by building up the letter sounds. Each side had its advocates who can point to studies which 'prove' the advantages of their chosen method. Observing my own children and the other children we know, I get the impression that there are benefits and drawbacks on both sides. Some children we know who learned by the 'look-say' method, having whole words pointed out to them with no teaching of letters, very quickly became fast fluent readers, apparently years ahead of their peers. I noticed, though, a couple of years later, some of the parents would comment that their children's spelling was not as brilliant as might be expected, bearing in mind their reading ability and interest. On the other hand, the children we know who learned by the phonic method, although off to what seemed a slower start in reading, were comparatively efficient spellers. I am sure I am not alone in making this observation.

Helping Hosanna to read, I did what came most naturally to me – drawing her attention to whole words in books, written messages, shop windows, road signs. I did not start to teach phonics until after school starting age but, as she had already mastered the art of reading, this was a process she found, not surprisingly, uninteresting. Her spelling trailed somewhat behind her reading but that seemed entirely to be expected. We were confident that it would click into place 't does, but it takes more time.

The question of spelling tempted me to try out the phonic method with Fiorin, just to see how that would work out. But when it came to it I found myself wondering whether it was not fine for phonetic languages like Italian, but too simplistic for English where the same

letter may have several different sounds. How could I tell a child that
e says 'eh' when most of the time it patently does not?

Instead, I have used a combined method with Fiorin, whole words
with phonics introduced as she learns to read, rather than after. It is
too early to see whether this will make any difference to the age at
which she will come to grips with spelling.

In her book, *Spelling Caught or Taught*, Margaret Peters describes
the good fast reader who flashes over words so quickly she does not
look at them long enough to notice how they are spelt. She
recommends slowing the reader down sometimes to give her a
chance to look at words. For this, she suggests reviving the practice
of listening to the child reading aloud – something many parents
drop when the child is a fluent silent reader. She makes other
suggestions for encouraging children to look at words. I thought this
was interesting – it is easy to see that those children taught phonically
are taught to *look*. As long as whole-word readers are encouraged to
look some of the time, I feel they should have the advantages of being
whizzy readers without the attendant disadvantage of not noticing
spelling. Most children will learn to read by either method. The
most important thing seems to me to be to foster enjoyment of
reading.

Reading Schemes   Adhering to a particular reading scheme is less
important with the whole-word approach, since the child adds to her
vocabulary as she meets words and does not have to be introduced
first to simple phonetic words which follow the rules.

The ubiquitous Ladybird reading books must be the reading
scheme most commonly used by parents teaching children to read.
Using them was the nearest we came to following a scheme, but we
skipped books at every level and used others as well. They are
inexpensive and widely available, in supermarkets and corner shops,
which has its advantages. Also, you do not need to order the whole
series from a bookshop, perhaps only to find yourself with books on
your hands that your child is not interested in. And what other
scheme can you pick up for a few pence at jumble sales? There are
workbooks and flashcards available. At each level the reading books
can be backed up (or substituted) by *Read It Yourself* books,
well-known stories retold with a graded vocabulary. I found these
were more popular than the basic Peter and Jane books.

There is a lot wrong with Ladybird books, but they have tried to
improve them. Peter and Jane now live on a housing estate; Jane
wears jeans and has tousled hair sometimes. However she still tends
to be looking on while Peter plays ball or climbs higher up the tree.
Active girls like Hosanna and Fiorin notice this sort of thing, but the
more recent versions are better than the old ones on this score. In our

house we still have not forgotten the classic line, 'Daddy reads and Mummy works' with the picture of Daddy sitting with the newspaper while Mummy bustles around wearing an apron. In the newer books Daddy can be seen washing up.

Books for Young Readers   After the earliest stages of the Ladybird scheme, we went on to the books by Arnold Lobel – surely the best story-teller for young children – in the *I Can Read* series. (Some of them are now in Puffins.) Not part of any graded reading scheme, they are a delight to read. I cannot praise them enough, especially *Mouse Tales*, *Mouse Soup* and the *Frog and Toad* books. They are well crafted, have just the right amount of pathos, no more, and were thoroughly enjoyed by all of us – marvellous, too, for adults to read aloud to smaller children.

Can I really be thinking of mentioning Tintin books? I shouldn't: there is a lot to disapprove of – too many guns for a start, for my liking – but they are wildly popular with the children we know, girls and boys. The good thing about Tintin – apart from the jokes – is the comic strip format with lower case letters. There is a much greater incentive to read word bubbles and find out what someone is saying than there is to read a page of narrative. A friend of mine taught her small daughter to read with them. She would read through, pointing out the words and her daughter would look out for certain words that she could read herself. She started with 'Snowy' and made dramatic progress from there: she very soon became a fluent reader. Before Hosanna could read properly, she would sit by herself, picking out the words she could read and the sentences she could remember while following the story through the pictures. Tintin in French is the next step for us.

Information Books   Unfortunately, there isn't room here for many book recommendations, but I must at least mention Usborne books. The range of subjects is impressive – from high technology (computers, electronics, space travel) to the beginnings of the world (prehistory, the ancient civilizations, archaeology) to modern languages and nature study. They are not textbooks but are aimed to enliven and engage the child's interest in a subject. This is their strength. *The Pocket Handbook to the Ancient World*, for example, gets read and looked at in bed at night by my children so often that it surprises me. The combined volumes are especially good value. On each topic, there are sometimes several different titles designed for different age-groups. The books are widely available in shops or direct from Usborne. If you want to see the full range without sending off for the catalogue (for which there is a charge) you could ask in a book shop if they have a catalogue you can look at.

School Books   There are many publishers of educational books. The Information Resource Centre can provide you with a list. We have found the Cambridge University Press have a particularly good range of books for secondary school level subjects. When requesting catalogues from educational publishers, indicate age-range and subjects interested in. Before ordering, check number of pages and size of book: this may be indicated in the catalogue. In my experience, school textbooks are sometimes disappointingly slim as well as expensive.

SCHOOLS BROADCASTING

Independent Television and B.B.C. Television and Radio transmit schools' programmes for pre-school age to 'A' Level. Teachers' notes and pupils' booklets to accompany the programmes may be ordered although, in our experience, they are not always essential. Postage is added onto orders of publications direct from the television companies – so order booklets through your local bookshop and save the postage.

Independent Television   Each company sends out its own Annual Programme with details of television for schools and colleges. Contact the company that transmits in your area.

B.B.C.   Some Radio secondary school programmes are transmitted at night and need to be recorded for day-time use.
   Details of B.B.C. Radio and Television for schools are available from the School Broadcasting Information Department.

STEINER EDUCATION

Information about Rudolf Steiner's approach to education is available from the Anthroposophical Society, who will also give details of schools, special schools, homes and residential communities for the handicapped and emotionally disturbed.
   A catalogue for mail order of books is available from the Rudolf Steiner Press.

WOODCRAFT FOLK

The Woodcraft Folk is a progressive organization for children, boys and girls, from the age of six upwards. As a voluntary organization, parental involvement and support is welcomed. Formed in the 1920s, it has been expanding particularly rapidly in recent years – there are currently about 600 groups throughout the country. As well as regular weekly meetings, there are outdoor activities, including hiking and camping.

The Woodcraft Folk aims to encourage children to become self-reliant, to think for themselves and to participate in decision-making. Racial and sexual equality is practised in the groups. World peace and disarmament are actively promoted: the motto of the Folk is 'Span the World with Friendship'. Its main financial support comes from the Co-operative Movement.

For those who have doubts about Baden-Powell's philosophy – for example, in *Scouting for Boys* he wrote that bees are 'a model community, for they respect their queen and kill their unemployed'! – the Woodcraft Folk will be a more satisfactory alternative to Brownies/Cubs/Scouts/Guides. In the Woodcraft Folk, boys and girls are not segregated, allegiance is not sworn to God and the Queen, there is more emphasis on democracy and less on obedience, no military-style organization – no church parades, salutes etc. Hosanna loves it. She now tells me she liked Brownies but always felt a sense of duty about going – something she never feels about Woodcraft Folk.

WORLD-WIDE EDUCATION SERVICE

The World-wide Education Service (W.E.S.) is part of the Parents' National Education Union (P.N.E.U.), an educational charity. The W.E.S. was established to help families who might otherwise face separation when one of the parents is employed overseas, perhaps in a country where suitable education facilities are not available. The W.E.S. Home School was designed to enable such parents to teach their children themselves and thus be able to keep the family together.

Families enrolling in the W.E.S. Home School are allotted a tutor who will provide advice and guidance, by correspondence or personal interview, backed by a team of advisors. The parent takes on the role of teacher: the system involves 'the creation of a school in the home'. A programme of work is provided and a suggested weekly timetable is included as a guide. The curriculum is broad, based on the acquisition of language skills – listening, speaking, reading, writing – and on practical experience and the environment in which the children find themselves.

The programme caters for children up to the age of thirteen and aims to give them the equivalent of a 'good' school education. The aim is for a high academic standard. The curriculum was officially endorsed in 1981 by the Department of Education and Science and recognized as enabling children to return to school – state or private – when appropriate. The W.E.S. expects children to go to school in time to study for public examinations. It is, perhaps, aimed at families who might not normally consider home education: those who accept the basic principles of schooling.

Single subjects – English, mathematics, humanities and science – are also available separately. There is a two-year nursery course for the under-fives, designed for parents and for those running nursery groups.

Although the W.E.S. is primarily intended for expatriate families, it is equally suitable for families in this country who wish there were some sort of general correspondence course available for school-age children. The fees are not low – but you are paying for unlimited guidance and support, a fully thought-out and structured education, rather than just for materials. It seems a good idea for parents who may not have the confidence to undertake their children's education wholly on their own and who might otherwise contemplate private school fees – with which the cost of the W.E.S. compares favourably.

Charlotte Mason   The underlying principles of the W.E.S. are those of the Victorian educationist Charlotte Mason – who advocated home education. She founded the Parents National Education Union, a body of parents who chose to educate their children themselves – the E.O. of its day, I feel. Today's W.E.S./P.N.E.U. has sought to reinterpret her philosophy in the light of modern circumstances, believing that schools are not as unenlightened as they were in Mason's time.

Some of her views on education are as valid today as they were a century ago: her books still make interesting reading. She believed that education should be an enjoyable experience for the child, a process in which the parent has a part to play. A child's ability and understanding should not be under-estimated or played down to. Children should have access to the best in art, music and literature. She emphasized the individuality of the child – 'children are born persons' – and the enthusiasm of parents and children that is so fundamentally a part of learning at home.

THE U.S.A.
GROWING WITHOUT SCHOOLING

The late John Holt wrote about children and the failure of schools to provide them with opportunities for real learning. His stimulating books have influenced many people in America and Britain. He was an eloquent advocate of home education. The movement he was so closely involved with, Growing Without Schooling, produces a bi-monthly magazine of the same name. Copies can be obtained from John Holt Associates in Boston, U.S.A., or, in Britain, they may be ordered through Education Otherwise.

Bibliography

Aries, Philippe: *Centuries of Childhood* trans. Robert Baldick, Jonathan Cape Ltd (1962)

Baker, Joy (see also Wilding, Frances): *Children in Chancery*, Hutchinson & Co. Ltd., London (1964)

Carey, Diana and Large, Judy: *Festivals, Family and Food*, Hawthorn Press, Stroud (1982)

Cobbett, William: *Advice to Young Men and (Incidentally) Young Women*, The Curwen Press (1930)

Cockcroft Committee: *Mathematics Counts*: Report of the Committee of Enquiry into the Teaching of Mathematics in Schools under the Chairmanship of Dr W.H. Cockcroft, H.M.S.O. (1982)

Cox, Catherine Morris and others: *Genetic Studies of Genius, Vol 11 The Early Mental Traits of Three Hundred Geniuses*, Stanford University Press, California, Harrap (1926)

Deakin, Michael: *The Children on the Hill*, Andre Deutsch (1972)

De Mause, Lloyd (ed.): *The History of Childhood*, Souvenir Press, London (1976)

Douglas, J.W.B. – *The Home and the School*, Panther, London (1964)

Edwards, Betty : *Drawing on the Right Side of the Brain*, Fontana (1982)

Freire, Paulo: *Pedagogy of the Oppressed*, Penguin (1972)

Hainstock, Elizabeth D.: *Teaching Montessori in the Home, The School Years*, New American Library (1971). Also available, *Teaching Montessori in the Home, The Pre-School Years.*

Hardyment, Christina: *Dream Babies, Childcare from Locke to Spock*, Jonathan Cape (1983)

Head, David (Ed.): *Free Way to Learning, Educational Alternatives In Action*, Penguin (1974)

Holt, John: *How Children Fail*, Penguin (1970)

—— *How Children Learn*, Penguin (1969)

—— *Teach Your Own*, Lighthouse Books (1981)

—— *What Do I Do Monday?* Pitman (1971)

Holt, Michael and Dienes, Zoltan: *Let's Play Maths*, Penguin (1973)

Howell, Arnold A. et al: *Mathematics For Schools, Teacher's Resource Book, Level 1*, Second Edition, Addison-Wesley (1979)

Hudson, Liam: *Contrary Imaginations*, Penguin (1966)

Illich, Ivan: *Deschooling Society*, Penguin (1971)

Isaacs, Susan: *Intellectual Growth in Young Children*, Routledge & Kegan Paul (1930)

Kent, Graeme: *What Should Your Child Know?* Harrap London (1983)

Mahony, Pat : *Schools for the Boys?* Hutchinson, London (1985)

Mason, Charlotte: The Home Education Series: *Vol I – Home Education, Vol 3 – Home and School Education*, Kegan Paul & Co (1886). Reprinted in 1955 by Scrivener Press.

Middleton, Nigel and Weitzman, Sophia: *A Place For Everyone, A History of State Education from the End of the 18th Century to the 1970s*, Victor Gollancz Ltd., London (1976)

Montessori, Maria: *The Secret of Childhood*, Longman (1936)

Moore, Raymond S. and Moore, Dorothy N.: *Better Late Than Early*, Readers Digest Press, New York (1975)

Mullarney, Maire: *Anything School Can Do You Can Do Better*, Fontana, London (1985)

Neill, A.S.: *Summerhill*, Penguin (1961)

Pestalozzi, J.H.: *How Gertrude Teaches Her Children, An Attempt to Help Mothers to Teach their own Children and an Account of the Method* trans. Lucy E. Holland and Frances C. Turner George Allen & Unwin Ltd., (1915)

Peters, M: *Spelling – Caught or Taught?* Routledge (1985)

Pollock, Linda A.: *Forgotten Children, Parent-child relations from 1500 to 1900*, Cambridge University Press, Cambridge (1983)

Ritter, Jean and Paul: *The Free Family: a Creative Experiment in Self-regulation for Children*, London (1959)

Rosenthal, Robert: *Pygmalion in the Classroom, Teacher Expectation and Pupils' Intellectual Development*, Holt, Rinehart and Winston, Inc. New York (1968)

Rousseau, Jean Jacques: *Emile*, J.M. Dent (1966)

Rusk, Robert R.: *The Doctrines of the Great Educators*, Macmillan, London (1969)

Steiner, Rudolf: *The Kingdom of Childhood*, Rudolf Steiner Press (1974)

Taylor, Geraldine: *Be Your Child's Natural Teacher*, Impact Books (1984)

Taylor, Isaac: *Home Education*, Jackson and Walford (1838)

Terman, Lewis M. et al: *Genetic Studies of Genius, Vol 1 Mental and Physical Traits of a Thousand Gifted Children*, Stanford University Press, George G. Harrap & Co.Ltd., London (1926)

Tizard, Barbara and Hughes, Martin: *Young Children Learning, Talking and Thinking at Home and at School*, Fontana (1984)

Valentine, C.W.: *The Normal Child*, Penguin Books (1976)

Van Der Eyken, Willem and Turner, Barry: *Adventures in Education*, Pelican (1975)

Vernon, P.E. (Ed.): *Creativity*, Penguin (1970)

Warner, Sylvia Ashton: *Myself*, Simon & Schuster (1967)

Wilding, Frances (Pseudonym of Joy Baker): *The House on the Hill*, Phoenix House Ltd., (1961)

Williams, E.M. & Shuard, Hilary: *Primary Mathematics Today*, Longman (1976)

Witte, Pastor C.H.G.: *The Education of Karl Witte*, Crowell Company, New York (1914)

Addresses

EDUCATION OTHERWISE

The reference library or Citizens Advice Bureau should have the address of your local Co-ordinator. The central address is:

Education Otherwise,
25 Common Lane,
Hemingford Abbots,
CAMBS PE18 9AN
Telephone: 0480 63130 (not after 9 p.m.)

The Education Otherwise Special Educational Needs Group is run by:

Sylvia Jeffs,
16 St Bernard's Road
Solihull,
West Midlands B92 7BB

ADVISORY CENTRE FOR EDUCATION (A.C.E.)

A.C.E.,
18 Victoria Park Square,
London E2 9PB

DISTANCE LEARNING

CORRESPONDENCE COLLEGES –

Wolsey Hall,
66 Banbury Road,
Oxford OX2 6PR

National Extension College,
18 Brooklands Avenue,
Cambridge CB2 2HN

EXAMINING BOARDS -

University of London

Entry forms for G.C.S.E. and G.C.E. examinations

The Secretary,
School Examinations Department,
66–72 Gower Street,
London WC1E 6EE

Regulations and Past Papers

Publications Office,
52 Gordon Square,
London WC1H OPJ

Associated Examining Board (A.E.B.),
Wellington House,
Station Road,
Aldershot,
Hampshire, GU11 1BQ

EDUCATIONAL SUPPLIES

E.J. Arnold & Son Limited,
Parkside Lane,
Dewsbury Road,
Leeds LS11 5TD

Hestair Hope Ltd.,
St Philip's Drive,
Royton,
Oldham OL2 6AG

James Galt and Company Limited,
Brookfield,
Cheadle,
Cheshire SK8 2PN

The Information Officer,
The Pre-School Playgroup Association,
61–63 Kings Cross Road,
London WC1X 911

INFORMATION RESOURCE CENTRE

Information Resource Centre,
A & D Anderson,
95 Derrington Avenue,
Crewe,
Cheshire CW2 7JA

MATHEMATICS

The Cuisenaire Company,
11 Crown Street,
Reading, RG1 2TQ

MONTESSORI

Montessori Society A.M.I. (U.K.)
26 Lyndhurst Gardens,
London NW3 5NW

London Montessori Centre,
18 Balderton Street,
London W1Y 1TG

St Nicholas Training Centre,
23–24 Princes Gate,
London SW7 1PT

MUSIC

The British Suzuki Institute,
21–23 London Road,
St Albans,
Herts AL1 1LQ

READING, SPELLING AND BOOKS

Usborne Publishing Ltd.,
20 Garrick Street,
London WC2E 9BJ

Cambridge University Press,
The Edinburgh Building,
Shaftesbury Road,
Cambridge CB2 2RU

SCHOOLS BROADCASTING

For information about Independent Television Schools Programmes contact the network that transmits in your area.

For information about B.B.C. Schools Programmes, contact:

B.B.C. School Broadcasting Information,
Villiers House,
The Broadway,
London W5 2PA

STEINER EDUCATION

Rudolf Steiner House,
35 Park Road,
London NW1 6XT

The Rudolf Steiner Press,
38 Museum Street,
London WC1A 1LP

WOODCRAFT FOLK

The Woodcraft Folk,
13 Ritherdon Road,
London SW17 8QE

WORLD-WIDE EDUCATION SERVICE

World-wide Education Service,
Strode House,
44–50 Osnaburgh Street,
London NW1 3NN

GROWING WITHOUT SCHOOLING

John Holt Associates,
729 Boylston Street,
Boston,
Massachusetts 02116, U.S.A.

Index

A.C.E. *see* Advisory Centre for Education
Access Studies scheme 97
Advice to Young Men (Cobbett) 162–5
Advisory Centre for Education 59, 115, 178, 196
A.E.B. *see* Associated Examining Board
Aims of Primary Education Project (Pat Ashton) 67–8
Alcott, Louisa May 165, 166
Artists, home education of 173
Ashley-Walker, Jude 125–7
Associated Examining Board 58, 197
Austen, Jane 169–71

Baker, Joy 69, 106
Ball, Betty 123–5
Bell, Vanessa 167–9
Better Late than Early (Moore, Raymond S. and Dorothy N.) 80–1
Bronte family 171–3
Burnett, Frances Hodgson 165

Cabinet Ministers 52, 55
Cameron, Lynette 98–9
Care Order 31, 102, 126
Casa dei Bambini 19
Chatterton, Thomas 156–7
Chiland, Colette 53
Child Benefit 98–9
Children: at home, coping with 15, 80–1, 125;
freedom of choice in learning 12, 44, 102, 118, 119, 137, 140–1;
growing at own pace 69–71, 149;
keeping responsibility for 11–12, 40, 79–80, 175;
labelled as failures 45–6, 47, 56–9, 96;
labelled subnormal or maladjusted 56–7;
loss of bloom 66–9;
registered but not attending school 111;
rights of 102, 150
Children in Chancery (Joy Baker) 69
Chorley, Primmy 120–3, 125
Cobbett, William 162–5
Cockcroft Report 184–5
Colleges: of further education 92, 97, 183;
library facilities 183;
technical colleges 84, 94, 95–6, 134, 183;
universities 96–7
Competition 92–3
Composers, home education of 173
Computers 83, 96, 132
Conform, pressure to 13, 66–7, 98, 118
Conversation as education 28, 32, 35, 57, 85–7, 120, 121, 124, 126, 127, 129, 138–44, 163–4, 168, 170
Correspondence courses 94–5, 132, 133–5, 191–2, 196
Cottage Economy (Cobbett) 162
Covenants 55
Cuisenaire rods 139, 186, 198
Curriculum: 38, 44, 109, 113, 114, 117, 124, 161
Cuts in education spending 49, 54, 58

De la Fontaine, Jean 157
Deregistration 106, 109–12
Deschooling Society (Ivan Illich) 56, 154, 155
Discipline 91, 119, 124
Distance learning 178, 191–2, 196
Douglas, J.W.B. 53
Downie, Lesley 128–9

Drawing on the Right Side of the Brain (Betty Edwards) 145
Dream Babies (Christina Hardyment) 174
Drugs and glue-sniffing 67
Dumas, Alexandre 157

Early Years 176
Edison, Thomas 157
Education A–Z (A.C.E.) 178
Education, idea of, limited by school 61
Education Act 1944 26, 30, 36, 52, 100, 101, 104–6, 108, 114, 175
Education Act 1981 115
Education Advisor 34, 35–9, 98, 112–4, 122–5, 127, 151–2
Education Otherwise 26, 30, 39, 64, 89, 96, 106, 107–8, 114, 116, 119, 125, 175–7, 196;
  accounts from members 118, 120–35, 177
Education Welfare Officer 32–34, 108, 111, 112, 113
Educational materials and supplies 81–85, 179–182, 197
Eliot, T.S. 70
Emile (Rousseau) 71, 91, 160, 161
E.O. *see* Education Otherwise
Equality of opportunity 93
Everdell, Nick 95, 133–5
E.W.O. *see* Education Welfare Officer
Examination, 11-Plus 53–54, 62
Examinations, G.C.S.E. and G.C.E.: 58–9, 94–7, 178–9, 182, 183, 197;
  'A' Levels: results 57–8, 62;
  ambivalence towards 130, 132–3;
  cost of 98;
  resources needed for 84;
  success at home in 132, 135;
  syllabuses, past papers 94, 183
Examining boards 57–9, 94, 196–7
Experts 50–1, 126

Farjeon, Eleanor 165
Fenelon 91
Files, school 59–60
Flexistudy 95, 179

Forgotten Children (Linda Pollock) 155
Forster, E.M. 90
Freire, Paulo 47
Froebel, Friedrich 161

G.C.E. and G.C.S.E. *see* Examinations
Genetic Studies of Genius, vol. 2 (C.M.Cox) 156
Goldsmith, Oliver 156
Growing Without Schooling 192, 199

Hainstock, Elizabeth 186
Halsey, A.H. 51
Hawthorne, Nathaniel 157–8, 168
History of Childhood (Lloyd de Mause) 154–5
Hollingworth, L.S. 70
Holt, John 60, 192
Home and School (Tyrrel Burgess) 106
Home education: cost of 97–9;
  flexibility of 18, 69–71, 136, 137, 139–41, 148;
  freedom from school worries in 49;
  hours required for 103–4, 109;
  in the past 154–73;
  isolation in 131, 141, 165–6, 171;
  objections to 25, 78–99, 117–8, 126, 135;
  problems during 88, 118–9, 126, 127, 130, 142–3, 177;
  producing evidence of 122, 126–7, 151–2;
  receptivity of children during 66–9;
  secondary years 132, 133–5, 151;
  self-directed learning 35, 47–8, 90, 118, 128–9, 133–5, 146–8, 157–8, 160, 163, 165–6, 168, 170, 171
Home Education (Isaac Taylor) 137
How to be a Gifted Parent (David Lewis) 86
Hunter, John 156

Illich, Ivan 56, 154, 155
Individual, needs of the 69–71, 124

Information Resource Centre 182, 185, 190, 198

I.Q. 53, 70

Isaacs, Susan 19, 22

Joseph, Sir Keith 103

Lamartine, Alphonse 157

Languages: language laboratories 95; tapes and records 95, 183

Laslett, Rena 129–30

Law: relating to home education 100–6; human rights 101; legal battles 106–9, 111, 177

L.E.A. *see* Local Education Authority

Lewis, David 86

Library facilities 94, 95, 182–3

Literacy problems 102–3

Local Education Authority: approval from 122–3, 125, 135, 152; children's rights 102; contact with 30–9, 83, 94, 102, 106–16, 122–5, 127, 132–3, 151–2, 176; expectations of 32; grants to low income families 98; frequency of visits from 114; obligations of 71, 104–5; recognition of home education by 98, 99; testing by 113–14; threats from 126

Locke 119

Malting House School 19

Mason, Charlotte 192

Mathematics 123–4, 138–9, 163–4, 184–6, 198

Mathematics for Schools (Fletcher) 185

Mill, John Stuart 159

Montessori, Maria: 17, 18, 19, 22, 144, 161, 173–4, 181, 186; Colleges 186, 198

Morris, William 119

Music 70, 142–3, 180, 186–7, 198

Myself (Sylvia Ashton-Warner) 152

National Extension College 178–9, 196

Neill A.S. 11, 12, 173–4

News from Nowhere (William Morris) 119–120

Northern Ireland, Education Act 1947 106

Nursery schools 22–25, 147

Open University 97

Parents: as experts on children 50–1; as models 87–8; demands on 88; contributing to school funds 55; keeping in touch with children 23, 49–50; loss of time of 78–9, 165; legal obligations of 100, 101, 105–6; qualifications of: *see* Qualifications

Pascal 158–9

Pestalozzi 161

Physical Education 69–70, 144–5

Play 117, 137, 163

Playgroup 19–22, 27, 147

Poetry 74–77, 127, 144

Pollock, Linda 155

Potter, Beatrix 165–6

Pre-School Playgroup Association 180, 197

Prospectuses, college and university 183

Psychologist, educational 57, 64–5, 125–6

Pygmalion in the Classroom (Robert Rosenthal) 45

Qualifications: 94–7; as mature student 96–7; of parents 9, 43, 81, 84–7, 102, 126

Questions, answering children's 86–7

Razzell, Wendy 130–3

Read, learning to 120, 183, 187–89
Real world: access to 12, 72–4, 85;
  school is not 43, 48, 85, 90–1
Religious Education 71–2, 139–40,
  141
Resources: 81–5, 177, 178–92, 198;
  of schools 54–5
Robbins Report 52
Rosenthal, Robert 44–6
Rousseau, Jean Jacques 71, 91, 119,
  136, 160–1, 162
Rural Rides (Cobbett) 163–4
Ruskin, John 156, 168

School: and grim reality 90–2;
  as a game of chance 46–7;
  as caretaker 41–2;
  as instrument of social
    control 60;
  boys in 64–5;
  bullying in 64–5, 93, 125–6;
  failure of 68, 89–90, 102–3;
  girls in 61–4, 87;
  hours spent in 24–5, 40–1;
  inequality in 52–5, 55, 93;
  not compulsory 100;
  private 52, 54, 55, 109;
  remedial 56–7;
  resources 54–5;
  social class in 54–5;
  streaming in 53, 55;
  suppresses children's
    confidence 67–8;
  withdrawing child from 109–12,
    117, 125–30
School attendance, ages for 50, 81,
  104
School Attendance Order 105
School Is Not Compulsory 176
Schooling, parallel to 104, 117, 122,
  125, 126–7
Schools' broadcasting 148–9, 190,
  199
Schools for the Boys? (Pat
  Mahony) 63
Sciences, resources needed for 84,
  132, 134
Scotland, Education Act 1980 106
Secret of Childhood, The
  (Montessori) 186
Sewell, Anna 165

Sexual inequality in schools 61–4
Single parent families 78, 131, 132
Socialization 16, 42–3, 141–2, 147,
  148
Special Education Handbook
  (A.C.E.) 115, 178
Special Educational Needs 98,
  115–6
Spelling 139, 187–88
Spelling Caught or Taught (M.
  Peters) 188
Steiner, Rudolf: 17–18, 22, 173–4,
  190, 199
Sullivan, Michael 68
Summerhill (A.S. Neill) 11, 12, 118
Suzuki Institute 198

Teach Your Own (John Holt) 60
Teachers: controlling
    discussion 85–6;
  expectations of 44–6, 63–4, 86;
  foibles of 23, 46–7, 88, 89–90,
    171
Teachers' centres 129, 183
Tennyson 158
Testing by L.E.A. 113–4
Television 12, 65, 148–9, 150
Timetable 38, 109, 114, 117, 133
Toys 73, 121, 150–1, 156, 172
Tutors, private 96, 109

University of London Examining
  Board 196–7

Warnock, Baroness 89
Watt, James 158
Wesley, John 159
Williams, Ursula Moray 165
Woodcraft Folk 141, 190–1, 199
Woolf, Virginia 167–9, 170
Wolsey Hall 178, 196
Women writers 165–73
Workbooks 138, 145, 185
World-wide Education
  Service 191–2, 199
Writing difficulties 128–9

Yeats W.B. 13
Young, Antonia 183
Young Children Talking (Tizard,
  Barbara and Hughes, Martin) 85